Margaret D. Gill is a scholar, critic and a published and performance poet who taught mainly fundamentals of written English and language argument at The University of the West Indies, Cave Hill Campus. Kamau Brathwaite describes her as "One of the very finest poets in the Caribbean – and not only in English. Brilliant (and therefore important) a literary critic as any (of the too few) writing out of the Caribbean today."

Twice winner of the Barbados Frank Collymore Literary Endowment Award, 1998 First Prize, and 2006 Second Prize to Kamau Brathwaite, Margaret Gill was an International Visiting Writer 2007 at Hong Kong Baptist University (HKB) and one of two adjudicators of the HKB English Poetry Writing Competition 2007. She now holds the designation of Honorary Fellow in Writing by HKB.

Her poetry has been anthologized in several works including the earlier *Bim* and the new *BIM: Arts for the 21st Century*; *Aftermath* subtitled the "Best of Third World Poets" 1974; the *Oxford Book of Caribbean Verse* 2005.

Her critical publications include: *Alternative Songs From the Kingdom of the Lilies* (1998 Frank Collymore manuscript), *Lyric You* (2000), *Machinations of a Feminist* (2021) and *Rich Man In His Castle, Poor Ones Take the Street: Integrating a 'Canonical' Text & Popular Culture: A Study of the Novel 'In the Castle of My Skin' by George Lamming* (1st edition 2013).

Margaret likes to record that her writing is influenced by the fact that her mother wrote and her father loved poetry and knew large tracts of it by heart, and that her first award for poetry was received when she was 14 years old, when she won second prize in the Shankar's International Children Poetry Competition in India.

keywords:

carnivalesque; grotesque body; festive speech; creole
narrative; gender; woman; carnival; knowledge system;
west indian novel; vernacular forms; popular culture;
orality

First Edition, June 2013
Caribbean Chapters Publishing

Second Edition, November 2021
Margaret D. Gill
Khary Training
carrington1ll@yahoo.com

ISBN: 978-976-96713-7-9 Paperback Edition

Cover Photography: Michael W. Browne
Photograph Location: Blackman's Bridge, St. Joseph, Barbados

Cover Design: Grafixx 2 Inc

Table of Contents

Author's Note

As I imagine many critics do, I come to a text with only a few questions of an investigative sort and a deep willingness to encounter it as though it were a real world. My questions, though they may be few, already start to remake the text according to my desires, my prejudices. Fortunately, the text remains alive in itself—whatever that may be—for me because of my desire to encounter it whole and real. The good thing about my desire as opposed to my questions is that my desire is a thirst for real knowing, a curiosity to see what I can see. Hence my desire is not arising from a realist or abstract or any special kind of imagination that I know consciously about, but from hopefulness and a deep interest in being taken up upon whatever wings of logic or disharmony I find. Thus, I am able to read the text from the inside out. As well, I know several of my fears, prejudices expressed through my questions as I am reading my way in.

The resulting encounter between me and the text is joyous and painful and instructive. Having read *In the Castle of My Skin* for so long to write sensibly and attractively about it, I understand why people can produce so many sermons from the same Bible. I journeyed with the children of Israel of the village of Creighton up to the Promised Land. For them it seems to me that promise is really in the castles of their good skin, all colour skin. Thumper makes it over and comes back with his head full of light but dressed like a clown, more light is evidently needed there. The boy G is about to cross over at the end of the book (others may have also gone ahead, like some of the women). One hopes (or maybe not) that it will indeed be to Trinidad and not a perceived necessary journey to England, but one suspects that he will have to take the long boat out to understanding. One wishes, really, that he indeed takes all remaining Creighton with him as indeed we all need (all colours in this our variegated Caribbean) to reach the Promised Land: the darkness just beyond the castles of each enclosing skin.

In Chapter one I develop the model I use to analyse the text and explore the context of the carnival masquerade in Barbados and Trinidad (two places where Lamming experienced these phenomena which I argue influenced the writing of Castle). I link these to the Penny Bank, a key metaphor of cultural/political resistance in Castle. I also link the carnival spectacle to other instances in the text in this chapter. I then apply the model to the text in respect of two Bakhtinian concepts, the grotesque body and comic speech or what I call creole narrative. These form the substance of chapters two and three. Chapter four extends the discussion on Creole narrative and examines the calypso aesthetic as a form of Creole narrative utilised in Castle. In the next chapter I consolidate the discussion on gender in this text which I touched on in previous chapters. This chapter owes its existence to the fact that women constitute a special presence in oral forms of popular culture and hence in Castle. The conclusion of my study follows in chapter six.

As an appendix I include an interview with the author that provides the last word in the study. This interview only became possible at the end of the research, but it allowed me to get the writer's feedback on aspects of the study. I asked Dr. Lamming a series of open-ended questions in two days of interviews to which he responded. In addition, he responded in the interview to issues from a version of chapter five on feminist discourse in the study which was published in a book edited by Eudine Barriteau entitled *Confronting Power, Theorizing Gender: Interdisciplinary Perspectives in the Caribbean*, 2003. I include only the taped and transcribed interview of the second day here since the first interview was un-taped. In the few instances where I quote Dr. Lamming drawing on his words in the un-taped interview, I do so drawing on my university Masters level training and professional experience in anthropological research methods.

On some issues my views and those of Dr. Lamming diverge, and his comments constitute an immediate critique of my work. Where possible I integrated his critique into my analysis. Where I disagree with him and see no resolution to our differences I allow my view to stand alongside his. I also allow for us to misunderstand each other in the interview as in my analysis here. I include the interview as a record in the unfolding of the ideas of this important Caribbean thinker.

Note: I refer to the author as Lamming, but wish to refer to the person as Dr. Lamming. I find it necessary to do this in order to accord a certain ceremony.

Acknowledgements

I give thanks to Jah for the will, energy, commitment and ultimately the capacity to complete this study.

I give thanks to my supervisor Dr. Curwen Best for his support and encouragement, and for that of Professors Connie Sutton and Tim Reiss of New York University. They supplied the spark that generated this study and kept me confident in my ability to do it whenever I faltered. Professor Reiss published a version of Chapter 4, the study on Lamming and calypso, in a collection he edited entitled: *Music, Writing and Cultural Unity in the Caribbean*, 2005.

I give thanks to friends and family, without whose constant blessings it would not have been possible. Among these I include Professor Kamau Brathwaite, also of New York University, Professor Eudine Barriteau for the opportunity of publishing the chapter on "Feminist Discourse in Castle" in an earlier form in the book she edited entitled: *Confronting Power, Theorizing Gender*. The rigor with which that book treats the concept of gender clarified much of my thinking on the issue. Dr. Elizabeth Best and Dr. Alana Johnson contributed ideas from their specialist fields. Drs. Stacy Denny and Korah Belgrave know of their contributions towards encouraging this effort. Their efforts were not small. My son Khary believed in me and so did Preston Melville, who debated ideas and shared his wide knowledge, especially on photography and photographic scholarship. My publisher Carol Pitt made the journey a valuable learning experience.

God knows I just give thanks.

List of Illustrations

Introduction

The aim of this study is to analyse George Lamming's first and key text, *In the Castle of My Skin* (hereinafter referred to as '*Castle*'), in the light of several popular culture texts. *Castle* reached its fiftieth anniversary in the year 2004. The novel represents a model and archetype for much of the West Indian literature of its time of emergence in the 1950s, and continues to do so for some of the literature, mostly written by women, coming out of this current period. After teaching a course on West Indian women writers at the Cave Hill Campus of the University of the West Indies between 1991 and 1993, Evelyn O'Callaghan's conclusions supported this connection (3-8). *Castle* is rendered more significant by the perceived interplay between this canonical text and certain vernacular and popular cultural forms.

This study seeks to understand how this literary text is formed by and intersects with dialect and oral traditions as knowledge systems. It reaches beyond describing features of oral culture existing in the scribed text, as this effort, while useful in providing information, does little to explain anything about reading and writing practices. Instead, the study views orality as a philosophic system that helps explain the text and the moments of social history that produces it and us as writers and readers.

Irene Joyce Middleton offers a concept that hints at what is explored here. As Middleton defines orality, it means a whole conceptual theory of language encompassing orally-based thought and expressions along with dialect and oral traditions (301). The significance of her concept is that it anticipates the recognition that orality constitutes an interpretive discourse in itself. It not only represents practices that exist as artefacts only to be discovered and described, but oral practices themselves offer ways of looking at a text that can open up previously elided or silenced experiences of the text and its formation. Additionally, using oral culture to explore the text in this way offers new insights on established critical practices themselves and how they discipline our understandings of what is significant to notice in and about texts, and about the inter-relations of texts with other aspects of culture.

Kamau Brathwaite rightly argues in *History of the Voice*: "To confine our definitions of literature to written texts in a culture that remains ital in most of its people proceedings, is as limiting as its opposite: trying to define Caribbean literature as essentially orature—like eating avocado without its likkle salt" (49). Brathwaite's 'ital' draws on Rastafari talk, the vernacular of followers of the Rastafari faith which was first founded by Afro-Jamaicans in the mid-nineteen thirties. He uses this apt word to define a culture that continues, despite the pressure and presence of the Western book, to be face to face and oral in much of its expressions and forms. This dominance of the oral culture is being even further augmented by the pressure being brought to bear against reading in many countries in the Caribbean by a growing audio-visual civilisation. Hence there is an even greater need to understand orality and how we re-present it and are re-presented by it.

Following the logic of Brathwaite's argument, it is equally limiting to imagine that the literature remains uninformed in a formal and philosophical sense by the oral culture. The force that oral culture in the Caribbean exerts against the culture of the book is such that it infiltrates and improvises on the latter: the written is necessarily bound up with the oral culture, and vice-versa. O'Callaghan uses similar logic when she argues that West Indian women writers draw on the resources of the oral tradition to inform formal aesthetic choices in their works (7). However, she confines this discussion to women writers. Carolyn Cooper gets closer to the approach taken in this study about the vernacular being a discursive system that illuminates the written text in her exploration of the uses of the Kumbla in Erna Brodber's novel *Jane and Louisa Will Soon Come Home* (279-288), but again she confines this discussion to a woman writer.

There is a continuum that deserves further exploration between the so-called high-culture canonical text and performance–

based texts which are perceived as so-called 'low culture'. There are similarities in major features of these texts, and if understandings normally reserved for the 'low' text are applied to the 'high', they will bring unique and so far unexplored but vital ways of reading the latter, and vice versa. These readings complicate the use of literature as a way of imagining West Indian identity and exploring social relations in the countries in the region. For example, it is possible to expand understanding of the novel *Castle* (and consequently its use in interpreting and promoting certain images of West Indian and Caribbean society) by examining its use of strategies of comedy, historical narrative and political invective normally used in the structuring of calypso.

Castle has been analysed for its relation to history and politics, but has never been assessed for its connection to calypso as a medium which itself also addresses concerns of history and politics, among other issues. The fact that the novel makes use of comedy as a structuring device has also not been examined. The connections point to the carnivalised nature of this literary text, to use Mikhail Bakhtin's term (qtd. in Morris 196). If examined in light of carnivalesque forms, it is clear that this text is fed by popular humour and images and topoi of popular culture. These complicate the meanings that can be derived from and about the text. These modes of thought exert pressure against the novel form and inform its meanings in ways that invite further investigation.

The methodology used is designed to suit the thesis of the study; hence it veers from orthodox practices. The study is not rooted in the conventional horizontal comparison of this novel with several other novels by different authors, although it makes some links with Earl Lovelace's *The Dragon Can't Dance*, and Jean Rhys' *Wide Sargasso Sea*. There are other West Indian literature texts which deal specifically with carnival or are rooted in other folk forms which may bear comparison. For example, there is Paule Marshall's *The Chosen Place the Timeless People*, which gives significant space to exploring the involvement by characters in a carnival masquerade. There is C. L. R. James's focus on yard life in his novel *Minty Alley*, and there are Erna Brodber's novels *Jane and Louisa Will Soon Come Home*, as mentioned earlier, and *Myal* with its explorations of folk medicine and religious forms and cosmology. Vertical comparison of *Castle* with Lamming's other novels which highlight certain folk forms is also not our focus. For example, *Season of Adventure*, with its concern with the steel pan, and *Of Age and Innocence*, which is built around a (fictional) folk tale, are both good candidates for future research using the methodology employed here.

This study compares *Castle* with other texts normally thought of as popular culture performances. These other texts include mainly folk songs, the calypso, folk tales, proverbs, comic theatre and street theatre or masquerade, and these are closely read for their theoretical structures and assumptions. *Castle* encapsulates features of these other modes of discourse, although the connections have hitherto been unexplored. It is hoped that the new ways of reading the novel offered by this comparative analysis will provide interesting and useful ways of reading other West Indian texts. The limited application of the methodology to *Dragon* done in this study is meant to explore what is possible in reading between two literary texts across the vernacular form.

The theoretical frame is informed mainly by several approaches taken by Kamau Brathwaite and Mikhail Bakhtin. Kamau Brathwaite's concepts of orality and the resisting "little tradition" (*Contradictory Omens: Cultural Diversity and Integration in the Caribbean*) are key informing constructs (30). Kamau Brathwaite, a Barbadian like Lamming, believes and has frequently argued that the folk tradition (the "little tradition") offers an alternative tradition that has always existed, though not without challenge and consequent change, in spite of slavery and colonial oppression (*Omens* 30). This alternative tradition deciphers and makes visible modes of domination, and resists attempts to dominate considerations of relevance by asserting alternative meanings and alternative social values. Mikhail Bakhtin's ideas about tradition, freedom and folk carnival aesthetic subversion which he explores in depth principally in his book *Rabelais and His World*, are also employed.

Bakhtin seeks to understand human behaviour, particularly in the use human beings make of language to establish power differentials and also to challenge them, and sees in the parody, caricature and other comic gestures of communal festivals of several European countries enactments which operate as a kind of language that seeks to oppose and dismantle conventional hierarchical culture (*Rabelais and His World* (39-40)). He sees this folk laughter as an important influence on classical traditions of writing in Europe and in particular examines how it affected the work of the novelist Rabelais.

I also draw on Richard Burton's modifications of Bakhtin's model by his introduction of the notion of a "carnival complex" (157) to better fit the model for my purposes, and on Curwen Best's tuk theory which offers a way of reading the scribed text according to the ensemble production of Barbadian tuk band music (*Popular Music* 14). *Castle* is an ensemble production that bears analysis using an assemblage of theoretical frames. The value of this approach is that it offers a re-visioning of popular culture and of classical West Indian literature and literary criticism. By so doing, it exposes the power relations that continue to constitute literature and literary criticism as cultural forms that maintain social hierarchies.

It seems appropriate to use the theories on alternative culture from below by Brathwaite and Bakhtin as a major frame for this study. Approaches by both Brathwaite and Bakhtin assert the primacy of intercultural accommodation as opposed to hegemonic force as the basis for the expression of national cultures, and hence for interpreting them. They both argue that one cannot understand culture from examination of only official cultures and their influence in shaping national cultures, but that one must consider unofficial modes that seek to assert themselves in the face of domination and exclusion. This proposes that the "little tradition" retains some power and agency, a view I fully support and offer even in understanding the forces that shape this novel.

Both Bakhtin and Brathwaite point to the hybrid nature of the subject and the importance of considering community in assessing that hybridity. This is a key principle of subjectivity to which vernacular forms testify and which is a principle that *Castle* upholds. By this understanding, the self transcends its limits and temporarily enters the space of the other, in order to offer the other and itself the possibility to achieve completion.

It also seems appropriate to use the models of both theorists instead of either one alone. Despite the fact that the two theorists investigate different cultural spaces, Europe and the West Indies, and emphasise traditions that originate one in Europe and the other in Africa, they both appear to be pointing to the same thing—how dominant cultures are made relative and de-privileged by the cultures of the dominated. In other words, they both point to the dialogic nature of culture. The use of these two theories to complement each other is justified in view of the fact that Lamming's *Castle* participates in both European and West Indian novelistic traditions. Bakhtin's model needs to be adjusted to more accurately fit the context of the Caribbean, and Brathwaite's model needs to be augmented to accommodate more of the carnival forms, as his emphasis is more on language issues. The model that emerges from putting the ideas of these two key theorists in dialogue seems suitable for a comparative analysis of *Castle* and West Indian vernacular forms. This approach fits more the intercultural nature of the region's social forms, especially the intercultural nature of the texts under investigation (Best *Popular Music* 14).

Brathwaite explores this concept of interculturation. In evaluating European impact on Caribbean space, he acknowledges that this led to the submergence of all other languages, and argues,

> "...this very submergence served an interesting interculturative purpose... [That] underground language was itself... moving from a purely African form to a form which... was adapted to the new environment and adapted to the cultural imperative of the European languages. And it was influencing the way in which [Europeans] spoke their own language. So there was a very complex process taking place, which is now beginning to surface in our literature" (*Creole Society* 309).

Bakhtin's concepts of dialogism and heteroglossia seem to offer a similar understanding: "The word is born in a dialogue as living rejoinder within it; the word is shaped in dialogic interaction with an alien word that is already in the object. A word forms a concept of its own object in a dialogic way."(Morris 76). As Michael Holquist cogently explains Bakhtin's idea:

> "...dialogism is the characteristic epistemological mode of

a world dominated by heteroglossia. Everything means, is understood, as a part of a greater whole - there is a constant interaction between meanings, all of which have the potential of conditioning others. Which will affect the other... is what is actually settled at the moment of utterance. This dialogic imperative... insures that there can be no actual monologue..." (426)

The history of European colonialism in the West Indies and resistance to it demonstrates the dialogic process. In their efforts to stabilise their imperialist project, European colonizers were committed to the dissemination of fixed negative representations of Amerindians, Africans, the indentured labour brought later from the Asian world and even the nature of the 'new world' itself. Their project described a centripetal monologic tendency, in other words. However, this centripetal force has been countered by the centrifugal force or dialogism represented in the submerged perspectives of the subjugated and enslaved 'Amerindians', Africans and their creolised descendants, and the other immigrant labour that came after emancipation. The challenges these submerged traditions bring fracture existing dominant paradigms and force them to accommodate alternative meanings and expressions. Bakhtin describes the process of such contests for meaning introduced by stratification and consequent heteroglossia as dialogization (Morris 75-76).

The hypothesis here is that evidence of such dialogism exists in the continuously evolving expressions of popular culture of the black Barbadian majority, which challenge forces and mechanisms of colonialism and neo-colonialism. It is argued that the written literature has taken up and expresses these contradictory forces. Because of its debt to the English language novel writing traditions, the literature expresses the tendency inwards into monologism, a tendency that canon-creating literary criticism has fed. However, its carnivalisation by the infiltration of popular culture expresses a movement outwards into dialogism.

Brathwaite introduces a concept similar to Bakhtin's notion of hybridity and dialogisation when he argues for the acknowledgment of a dichotomous cultural landscape shot through with tendencies towards creolisation. By creolisation he means creative interculturation that balances a strong force towards imitation of European values with a commitment to folk norms (*Omens* 16). Brathwaite, to my mind, models this complex response in his recuperation of the "Uncle Tom" figure, traditionally seen by colonial eyes and the eyes of his children as figure of shame and ridicule that accommodates and imitates European values. Brathwaite insists that this character be acknowledged as a valuable ancestor or strategy of resistance. In a poem in "Rights of Passage" in the trilogy *Arrivants: A New World Trilogy* Tom says:

> "So to New York London
> I finally came
> hope in my belly
> hate smothered down

> to the bone
> to suit the part
> I am playing.
>
> And I should like to see
> my children's children
> slender shoots: the grow
> ing green reminders
> of the seeds I gave..." (22)

In other words, Uncle Tom plays the part in order for his progeny to survive the holocaust of slavery. He sacrifices himself to the cross of ridicule and shame rather than be lost in the self-glory of immolation of the plantation and himself. This way, he can remain to teach the values of forgiveness, spirituality and hope to his progeny. Importantly though, he harbours in reserve the "hate smothered down to the bone", which is a value that may also become necessary to pass down. In the meanwhile, forgiveness, spirituality and hope are the values that Tom believes will ensure his progeny's survival over the long haul, if they are to remain human beings under a system that attacks the very roots of their humanity.

Another Barbadian poet, Bruce St. John, supports Brathwaite in this position of acknowledging pragmatic interculturation. St. John, speaking initially about slavery in Barbados but drawing correspondences with modern Barbados, says:

> "...when there are no huge mountains, no large rivers, no jungles, and sea hugs the land closely, revolt is difficult, running away is impossible;... [r]evolt will come but as an

explosion. In the meantime, a buffer must be found. The Barbadian is humour,... a humour in which irony abounds." (26)

He says further in the same text:

> "In addition to humour, oppressed peoples often have to resort to silence as a method of communication, but this for the most part accompanied by gesture, grin, sigh, smirk, smile or simper... [They invest] simple words and sounds of the imposed language with multiple meanings." (28)

In her novel *Brown Girl Brownstones*, Paule Marshall's validation of the character Suggie can be read as another example of the hybridity which Brathwaite and St. John here identify, and which Lamming signals in his validation of certain folkways (Gill *Room* 20). Paule Marshall is a second generation Barbadian whose parents had migrated to the United States of America. In this novel, Marshall makes the other women perceive the character Suggie as too free with her sexual favours (209-210). As a consequence, the fictional Barbadian migrant community rejects her. However, Suggie can be seen as embodying, literally, the values of freedom and the natural joy of personal connection associated with the oral culture and back home. This is contrasted with the narrow, cold individualistic pursuit of material success symbolised in the desire by most of the other characters to acquire a brownstone house in America.

Therefore, for Brathwaite, Marshall, St. John, and it will be shown here for Lamming, the oral culture is absolutely vital in understanding the complexity of Barbadian interpretations and expressions of self. It is important to note also that this culture has its foundation in the body, though this is not to mean that it is not still rooted in intellectual and reflective process.

The third construct that is important for this study is orality as a representation of consciousness. The concern with orality addresses the question of the fashioning of a language to explore and express West Indian/Caribbean identity in a sphere where the dominant language available for use is that of the imperial 'centre'. However, while a concern with language has been central to many analyses of Caribbean literature, the exploration of the oral culture outside of language still has to be investigated in depth. As Barbadian scholar Curwen Best suggests, "the greater body of critics in this area of Caribbean arts have (sic) not come to respect and acknowledge [it]... as a true, deserving part of and correlate to the tradition... called 'West Indian Literature'" (*Popular Music* 19).

Kamau Brathwaite started to explore the phenomenon of orality in the context of West Indian literature in a debate he started in a 1971 special issue of his journal *Savacou*, entitled "New Writing." In this journal issue he examined the contributions of oral poets of the West Indies. He further developed it in his conceptualisation of 'nation language' in a critical exploration called *History of the Voice* which was published in 1984. In this he sought to theorise about the oral/scribal connection in Caribbean poetry. Since these, only a few published studies have pursued this concept of orality in West Indian literary and cultural studies. An important collection of papers exists in an edited book by Stewart Brown, which were presented at a conference entitled "The Pressures of the Text: Orality, Texts and the Telling of Tales" which was sponsored by the Centre of West African Studies, University of Birmingham in May 1995 (The Pressures of the Text: Orality and the Telling of Tales). Most studies in this frame have taken as their unit of analysis the literary text, and excavated it for its oral artefacts and tendencies (Brown *Mama Lola*; Rohlehr *Strangled City*); others have turned to the 'oral' text and made their exegeses and theoretical excursions there (Cooper *Noises*; Best *Popular Music*). Most studies have followed Brathwaite's lead in refusing the easy dichotomisation of the concepts of oral/scribal, by preferring to challenge the validity of and ideological investments that inhere in both the categories as well as their discursive construction as binary opposites. According to Glyne Griffith:

> "[Brathwaite's notion of] nation language is in attempt to redress the imbalance precipitated by the Western emphasis on the scribal... Brathwaite is cognisant of criticism's need to find a balance between the oral and scribal. He does not merely reverse the configuration which privileges the scribal over the oral by fetishising orality, but argues for a balanced approach..." (11, 12).

The study of orality in the exploration of *Castle* is intended to advance this area of study. However, it is not limited only to questions of dialect or folklore, but is assessed as a set of distinctive goals, assumptions and manoeuvres, a distinctive world view which informs popular culture and literature in the sense in which the quote from Joyce Irene Middleton used earlier defines it. This way of understanding orality as a whole conceptual theory of language encompassing orally based thought and expression, and reconciling it with the written text, will expand the possibilities of observing resistance to colonial pressures and confinements, and will advance knowledge of how subjectivity is articulated or defended. Edward Glissant appears to be referring to this when he talks of the need for a new baroque (250). He says, "For us, it is a matter of ultimately reconciling the values of the culture of writing and long-repressed traditions of orality." (249) He continues, "It is the unknown area of these relationships that weaves, while dismantling the conception of the standard language, the 'natural texture' of our new baroque, our own. Liberation will emerge from this cultural composite." (250)

Barbadian subjectivity as expressed in *Castle* is neither monolithic nor exclusionary. Self is fraught with contradictions, hopes and possibilities, just as in the case of Brathwaite's Uncle Tom. The identity problem of the nation in *Castle* is one of enabling the preservation of diverse identities as much as it is about 'recuperating humanhood' and resuscitating a specifically oppressed African identity. As we are all aware, the latter in particular has been a major mission of Brathwaite's earlier work. The project of putting diversity in dialogue is modelled by many Barbadian writers besides George Lamming and Kamau Brathwaite. Paule Marshall, Bruce St. John, and Jeanette Layne-Clarke make orality an informing principle of their work in their persistent interest in double voices and heteroglossia. This concern also represents the modal expression of the carnivalesque.

This analysis is very applicable to understanding Barbados and Barbadian cultural forms compared to many other Caribbean countries, given the difficulty of practicing physical maroonage in a small country and in the context of the centralisation of British culture over a period of 339 years between settlement and political independence in 1966. In this flat landscape which was dominated by plantation and Anglican Church, maroonage, a process through which a little tradition could be nourished, would have been a response of the imagination and other non-physical arenas. These arenas include the language of the body that is expressed in street and other carnivalesque performances as it also includes language itself. As Kamau Brathwaite says in an argument that holds particularly true for Barbados and probably explains the persistent and very notable use of profanities in much regular Barbadian street talk,

> "...it was in language that the slave was perhaps most successfully imprisoned by his masters; and it was in his (mis)-use of it that he perhaps most effectively rebelled. Within the folk tradition, language was (and is) a creative act in itself; the word was held to contain a secret power..." (*Creole Society* 237).

It is from these non-official sources that Lamming draws models to develop and give meaning in his novel *In the Castle of My Skin*.

1 Carnival / Marketplace Masquerade and Castle

George Lamming's novel *In the Castle of My Skin* (*Castle*) has been appropriated as high culture West Indian literature, as its canonisation in West Indian literary criticism and academia demonstrates. However, a continuum exists between this 'high-culture' literary text and popular cultural texts existing in Barbadian and West Indian society at the time of its production. Mikhail Bakhtin's theories of carnivalised literature provide a good framework for understanding how key characteristics of carnival spectacle or popular marketplace-type activities of Barbados and the West Indies frame Castle. In this chapter it is argued that Castle aligns itself with the carnival as a model of post-colonial textual practice.

Bakhtin's model offers several important theoretical constructs which enable this exploration, especially when modified along the two important ways suggested by Richard Burton, that is, extension and intensification of carnival time. Given the concern of Lamming's text with utopian topics of freedom, transition and optimism, it yields well to application of the

Bakhtinian model. Lamming's investigation of the postcolonial situation via many of the forms described and presented by Burton validate use of his constructs in this chapter. It is on the basis of this theoretical frame that it is argued that carnival performance forms the matrix from which Lamming's Castle is moulded. Carnival performances supply the popular narrative structures that institute the West Indian novel.

Bakhtinian Carnivalesque

Castle annexes the radicalism and utopianism inherent in the carnivalesque as a point from which to explore identities and social formations alternative to the limiting templates of colonialism, and persistent class and race hierarchies. This carnivalesque phenomenon expresses itself in *Castle* via three Bakhtinian categories: the grotesque body, ritual spectacles of the marketplace and festive speech (Morris 196). These expressions of the carnivalesque, when applied to a reading of Lamming's *Castle*, expose its intermediary and heteroglossic nature. They also offer new insights on several of the author's choices regarding his narrative practices, location of action and character behaviour and psychology.

From his research of the long tradition of folk cultural forms in Europe, particularly in the middle ages, and its influence on French writer, Francois Rabelais, Bakhtin explains that the carnival spirit is an enactment by the folk which gives importance to what he calls the "material bodily principle," a "triumphant, festive principle" (*Rabelais* 19). Through and by this principle the folk deride, overturn and hence make relative the official speech and culture of authority—that is, they make them lose their authority status. The material bodily principle, imaged in the metaphors of the sensuous grotesque body, the feast, ritual spectacles of the marketplace and carnival laughter, provides the people with a "second life" (Bakhtin *Rabelais* 10). This life, Bakhtin asserts, represents "temporary liberation from the prevailing truth and from the established order; it mark[s] the suspension of all hierarchical rank, privileges, norms, and prohibitions" (*Rabelais* 10).

An important characteristic of the carnival spirit for Bakhtin is its complex nature. A collective rather than individual response, the carnival spirit of irreverent laughter is universal in that it is directed at anyone (even the carnival participants themselves) and it is ambivalent. The complexities described find clear expression in Bahktin's concept of the grotesque body which is characterized by its materiality and open-endedness (*Rabelais* 19). Specifically, the lower body is emphasized—the genital reproductive organs, the belly, the buttocks. The concern is therefore with eating, copulating, pregnancy, fecundity, and defecating. These acts represent the body's openness, its excesses, but importantly also its capacity to renew itself. These characteristics therefore relate the body to the flux of the self-renewing cosmos, Bakhtin proposes, and hence give it (the body) a utopian and radical nature (*Rabelais* 19).

This notion of the utopian nature of the material bodily principal of carnival, David Wiles argues in an essay on "The Carnivalesque in *A Midsummer Night's Dream*" represents the classical Platonic notion of carnival (61). As Wiles explains, Plato posited that the gods pitied the suffering human race and gave religious festivals to human beings as periods of rest and "so that men might restore their way of life by sharing feasts with the gods" (Wiles, 61). The characteristic of ambivalence, Bakhtin suggests, following the Platonic vein, means that although the carnival laughter denies and mocks, it also revives and renews. In this sense, the carnival spirit is utopian—it asserts a whole world, a realm of community, freedom, equality and abundance.

Contrary to the utopian view, the Aristotelian "safety valve" theory of carnival argues that the life of carnival is a mere release or catharsis which ultimately reasserts the existing status quo of hierarchies—religious, political and moral values, norms and prohibitions (Wiles, 62). While the utopian theory says that carnival is indicative of and seeks to restore an autonomous and historically progressive popular culture, the safety valve theory sees it as ultimately accommodationary, a kind of false consciousness that is eventually absorbed in the very states it seemingly opposes (Wiles, 63). Bahktin rejects the Aristotelian view of carnival in his valorizing of the body's open-endedness. This bodily principal is not 'allowed' by a hierarchical order that shows itself as ultimately viable by its capacity to accommodate even spurts of disorder. Rather, this principal cannot be contained as witnessed by its longevity.

Critical Responses to Bakhtin

It is necessary to note that some important on-going scholarship has opposed some of Bakhtin's theories. In a survey of critiques, Wiles notes that one argument is that Bakhtin generalises the concept of carnival although his references are specific only to the Mardi Gras (64). Another argument is that Bakhtin assumes that carnival is an autonomous cultural phenomenon that is always under popular control and has been resistant to change over time (Wiles 65). Thirdly, contrary to Bakhtin's assumptions, interpretations of what is 'grotesque' may be quite culturally determined according to an analysis by Wolfgang Keyser referenced by John Clement Ball (123).

While the above are important caveats, they do not necessarily negate critical principles in Bakhtin's theories. Bakhtin's notion of the body being grotesque is related to the disproportionate emphasis being placed on its physicality during carnival. During non-carnival times, the body is de-emphasised, as social congress stresses the personality/mind. However, in carnival time the unclosed/unclothed body finds expression, and is thus socially defamiliarised because exposed publicly within the brackets of the festival. Therefore, while Bakhtin is interested in the body's relationship to food during carnivals his interest is not mainly in this, but rather in its social 'ugliness'. That is, his main concern is in the body made 'strange'/socially unacceptable.

With respect to the second critique mentioned above, while the cooptation of popular festivals or popular rites by the elite does happen, this does not necessarily negate popular autonomy, precisely because of the process of re-inventing going on in popular activities. Through such re-inventions, as we shall see below, the many keep their cultures relevant and appropriate for their needs, including the need to resist attempts to appropriate and dominate meaning by hegemonic groups. An example of this in the case of Barbados will suffice.

Research by Terry Castle on masquerades in England suggests that the English, who settled in Barbados and formulated themselves as an elite class, would have had the experiences of actual masquerades and the representation of them in texts to draw on in formulating cultural practices and identities for themselves in the colony (2). Here in Barbados, these colonisers appropriated the festival called 'Harvest Home' held in England and Scotland to celebrate the gathering of the corn before the rains came, and introduced it in Barbados to celebrate the harvesting of the sugar cane (Liverpool 115). However, while in England this was a popular event marked by common feasts, speechmaking, singing and tournaments shared between rich elites and common people such as blacksmiths, wheelwrights, and parsons, in Barbados the local elites leached it of its more unruly and egalitarian aspects and presented it as another cultural practice that demonstrated white cultural superiority.

As Hollis Liverpool, a Trinidadian festival scholar records, "in Barbados, the English... did not invite the Africans to their tables nor display the kind of class tolerance and social levelling granted (sic) to poorer whites in England, but they encouraged the enslaved Africans with rum and extra allowances to dance, sing and parade" (116). However, Barbadian popular cooptation (or re-appropriation) of these festivities would reinvent the festival into a rite to serve the interests of the African population.

African Barbadians quickly appropriated these revels and added their own remembered African masks and dance celebrations. It is commonly understood that Africans had also brought their own festivals to the region, of which, despite the cultural devastation of slavery, they continued to practice remnants. In these celebrations they adapted whatever forms and means were possible and available to serve their needs not only for entertainment, but for freedom and resistance to domination and cultural unification by white Europeans. In Barbados, according to historian Marcia Burrowes, during the process of celebrating and rejoicing over the in-gathering of the crop as far back as the 1870s, labourers engaged in "marchings and dancing" to the playing of drums and the penny whistle or the flute (220). This was the nascent cultural form of the Barbados Landship with its decorated naval costumes and instrument-playing 'tuk' bands which by the 1930s, its heyday, was to occupy the streets, "gain[ing] access to key areas of colonial space" as a masquerade during holiday periods (Burrowes, 229).

What is also important to note for the purposes of this study is that the Landship movement, which at the time occupied the place of a carnival spectacle in Barbados, also played the role as a Friendly Society or savings society for poor Afro-Barbadians (Downes "Sailing... History of Land Ship" 93-122 and Downes "Searching... History of Landship" 64-78), and this is the model for the Penny Bank and Saving's Society in the novel *Castle*. My research identified that the largest of the Landships existed in Carrington's Village, the place where Lamming grew up, and in our un-taped interview, to the question about his experience of the Landship and Friendly Society, he agreed that he was influenced by it. He said "...the Friendly Society was everywhere. It was the source of the Penny Bank [in the novel]. People would have used it to meet their savings needs. They were important financial institutions created by the people." (02-08-2005)

Thus the people, through these two institutions, the Landship and the Friendly Society, appropriated and re-invented the elite carnival celebration. Furthermore, through them they captured physical space and also the economic space of finance, and turned them into their own marketplace spectacles. In clear recognition of the significance of this popular move and in an attempt to re-contain it for a great part of its history in the early 1900s, a campaign was launched against the Landship and Friendly Societies by the then Governor Hodgson (Downes "Sailing" 107-109). Hodgson, it is recorded, co-opted the police and Registrar of Friendly Societies to eliminate Landship Friendly Societies, and did so with great success in the case of many individual ship-societies (Downes "Sailing" 107-109; Burrowes 221). Lamming, in the taped interview with the author, says he recalls that such persecution existed. He recalls being told by an official on the bench that members of the judiciary sensed that there was a political thrust to the Landship and were moving to ban it, if not for the pragmatic intervention of the merchants. The latter benefited from the considerable profits they made from the large number of ships existing and the considerable amount of cloth they bought to make their costumes (Lamming, 10 Aug. 2005).

In using the model of the Lanship's savings society to represent a possibility of freedom from colonialism for Creighton Villagers, Lamming carried its carnivalesque notions of resistance, opposition and equality in the Bakhtinian sense into *Castle*.

Time in Bakhtin's Model

One of the qualifications of Bakhtin's model has to do with how time is treated within it. This qualification arises from another critique being brought to Bakhtin's theory by Richard Burton, writing of the carnival in Trinidad. His argument is that one has to speak not of carnival, but of a **carnival complex**. Burton's theory is that the carnival represents a "ritual of intensification," a concept he borrows from Nancy Sheper-Hughes (Burton 157). For Burton, the carnival does not stand as a polar opposite to non-carnival time, but represents an extension and intensification of a normal oppositional ethic that is expressed in carnival-like ways (157).

The notions of extension and intensification of carnival time are important additions to Bahktin's theory from the Caribbean perspective. While not completely un-bracketing carnival time, this way of posing the question asks that carnival time be seen as having important continuities with 'normal' time, where other forms of expression operate that voice similar challenges to authority as those posed through the carnival. In the same light, one has to re-examine apparently tame or mundane forms of cultural activities and personal expressions in day-to-day life to see where carnival ethics obtain. This has implications for analysis of other West Indian novels, since the issue is not whether actual carnivals are referenced, but whether these other forms organise narrative structures.

Burton's concept of a carnival complex rightly leads him to this radical re-examination of other activities which bear significant resemblances to carnival. Centring on the main characteristics of carnival, its play and reversal aspects, he identifies several such performances where dedication to pleasurable activity has also been turned to political ends. Here Burton points to tea meetings, Christmas 'mummings', ritual speechmaking and street arguments, the trading of boasts and insults in rum shops and the game of cricket (157). He argues that these performances mimic the forms of stylised display and combat which are intensified in the Trinidad carnival, and I add the Landship and Crop Over celebrations in Barbados, and certain other folk forms including comic theatre.

It is clear to see why Burton includes some of his activities. It is because of their inclusion of masking, eating and drinking and general display, and their connection to ritual threat and disturbance of the existing social order in whatever situation. In the case of 'Christmas mummings', activities which occur in several countries of the windwards and leeward island territories, revellers don simple costumes and go from house to house indulging in much eating and drinking. This tradition refers back to the English tradition of mumming which shares many of the same characteristics with the West Indian counterparts. Curwen Best identifies how in Barbados revellers ritually and volubly, but ultimately in jest, threaten to "mash down" the gardens of the residents of the houses they are attempting to enter for food and drinks (qtd. in *Barbadian Popular Music* 55). These revellers also seek coins for their performances, emphasising their right to be paid for the enjoyment they bring householders in the form generally of singing and, in the case of the tuk band performers of Barbados, drumming, and playing of whistles and steel triangle of the band. However, this tradition is specific to a particular season.

Cricket Carnival

Specific also to a particular season, but nevertheless bearing for Burton the transgressive ethos, stylised display and combat that are identified with carnival is cricket in the West Indies. Having been brought to the West Indies by the English and originally played only by elite whites, the game of cricket was to come to symbolize a spirit of resistance and national and regional independence for Blacks and later Indians as these West Indian under-classes sought to dominate at the game. Its conjunction with carnival has to do with the performers and spectators occupying spaces (as carnival revellers do the street) which are normally out of the control of the masses, and the reversals that the dominated effect as they uncrown the dominant group and make themselves equal to it. In their occupation of these denied spaces and their assertions of excluded and suppressed identities, the masses register their resistance to discipline.

C. L. R. James' ground breaking text, *Beyond a Boundary*, makes the successful argument that others have supported (Hilary Beckles and Brian Stoddart *Liberation Cricket: West Indies Cricket Culture*) that West Indian struggles against imperialism, racism, colonialism, and for independent and liberated self-hood mirrored the struggles fought by Blacks in the domain of cricket. Beckles argues that "West Indian inhabitants have sought to define their own existence in terms of an appropriation of space that could be autonomously manipulated in the building of discrete realities of freedom,... [and] cricket... represented an ideological and cultural terrain on which this very intensive battle was fought" (248).

James, Beckles and Stoddart, among other cricket historians, have shown how the struggles were fought and won, first to be included in the game, then to play on the side of the West Indies team, to have or belong to local clubs or sit in the players' pavilion, and to hold captaincy without and then with tenure. They have also identified how in winning these battles and then ensuring two long decades of unbeaten world leadership between 1976 and 1995, Black West Indians then changed the way the game was played and watched. The rejection of the ideological position held by white West Indian cricketers and administrators that a game against England was a non-political game between cousins, the innovative use of four pace bowlers, the refusal of crowds at matches to maintain any low-keyed decorum, all established a black identity for West Indian cricket and buttressed constructions of alternative identities by Black West Indians. While the term 'calypso cricket' no doubt was used to shore-up bigoted race-based views held by English commentators on West Indian style, it can also be seen as an accurate appellation which gets to the heart of the transgressive carnival ethic.

In summary, the non-traditional 'carnival' activities Burton identifies and which are discussed above and actual West Indian carnivals and the Crop Over masquerade share features of the ritual of rebellion or rite of reversal in the Bakhtinian terms. However, these activities are seasonal and are more easily identifiable with play albeit also with subversion. Similar to these, though less structured and regulated, are the street brawls and the trading of insults in rum shops which Burton also recognises as subversive carnival play. To these I add 'lickmouth', or 'old talk' in markets, and other community collection points such as stand pipes, spaces under trees, in shady spots next to houses, in barber, shoe repair and tailor shops, and in the establishments of other community service providers such as joiners and hair dressers where display, reversals and subversive play are also often present.

While not necessarily combative in the sense of being opportunities for trading insults or street brawls or even cricket stuggle, these occasions of community talk that are prevalent throughout the West Indies enable participants to air their views on any issues, including those in the purview of dominant groups or officials from which under-classes are officially debarred. An example of such an issue is the question which arises in *Castle* of the ownership of land in the plantation tenantry system that characterizes Creighton village. This issue becomes the centre of discussions at several of these 'marketplace' areas where community members gather. These occasions are often subversive in a political sense both at the level of personal as well as collective politics as they are in respect of this land issue. The *Dictionary of Caribbean English Usage* by Richard Allsopp defines 'lickmouth' and 'old talk' as gossip, or more accurately, as social talk that includes discussion of topics or issues of the day (415). In other words, something political happens as those down below occupy the denied space of ideology formation just as the people capture the streets in carnival. Several of these occasions or carnival marketplaces occur in *Castle*, where important community visions and alternative views and actions are explored.

Limitations of the Burton Model

It might be necessary to challenge important aspects of Burton's argument. He proceeds in his argument with a strict binary categorization that locates women and men within his schema as polar opposites (158). This placing implies that women are to private, inside and respectability, as men are to public, outside and reputation. Burton borrows the concept 'reputation' from Peter J. Wilson to denote the constant struggle for 'name' and recognition by men from the under classes in the Caribbean as a way of asserting identity (Burton 158). However, although the church in the West Indies is an official and popular public space, it is dominated by women as worshippers. Similarly, the literal marketplaces or the marketplace of the street masquerade in the Caribbean are definitely public domains, but again, they too are dominated by women.

Given the important place of these two institutions—the church and market—in any discussion of carnival or resistance by popular culture, the efficacy of Burton's model appears compromised. The official church in the Caribbean generally locates itself as contra the goings-on of carnival play. (Even the 'unofficial church' does this too, although as we shall see, the religious practices of the people 'down below' feature many of the elements of what we can call the carnivalesque.) On the contrary, the literal market place or the masquerade as a marketplace spectacle is a key site where popular culture contests for dominance. Of course the marketplace in the sense of the economy is a site where the official culture dominates, but here too in the Caribbean, popular culture contests for space in the significant presence of the informal economic sector and in the large numbers of the unemployed and consequent growth of the hustle and illegal economies as people seek to meet their needs and desires in the absence of secure, stable incomes (Gill *Women Work and Development* 18-19).

As it stands, Burton's use of the distinctions of public and private offer no improvement on or valid critique against Bahktin's model. Nevertheless, bearing these difficulties with the model in mind, it is still possible to accept the important concepts of extension and intensification, and hence continuity between carnival and non-carnival time which he offers as an advancement of Bahktin's ideas. It is possible to dispense with his discussion on men and women and still see value in his concepts of extension and intensification.

Marketplace Spectacle in *Castle*

As a result of their representation of significant cultural and political junctures, the marketplace spectacle spaces in the text (as in reality) are important sites where community issues and political actions are explored. These moments in *Castle* become vital centres of tension that energise the text and help us to see how Lamming explores constructions of Barbadian identity through forms of carnival play and display. Two such moments occur at the beginning of the text when Lamming is establishing the village itself as a character in the text.

The first moment which can be seen as a symbolic carnival happening occurs in the opening scene of the book and focuses on the rains. Although the villagers and the Mother insist that the rains are showers of blessing, the floods which these engender are not benevolent. The boy G likens the flood to the Biblical waters "which had once arisen to set a curse on the course of man. As if in serious imitation of the waters that raced outside, our lives—meaning our fears and their corresponding ideals— seemed to escape down an imaginary drain that was our future" (Lamming *Castle* 2). It is not difficult given this interpretation by G to liken the flood to the colonial condition that bedevils the villagers. How they respond to the flood signals the response that is modelled in the Penny Bank and Savings Society—they evince a collective response that is located deep in their cultural practices that can be conceived in terms of the carnivalesque.

The author makes the houses permeable to each other and to the outside public spaces under the rain/colonialism in that erasure of bodily boundaries—the open-ended body—that Bakhtin identifies as a carnival trait. This permeability of the houses is suggested by the seepage of the drenching rain through cracks and aged shingles, but this onslaught is met by the singing started by the protagonist G's mother (3). In a peculiar collective act, the inhabitants of the other houses take up her singing, and it is as though the houses fuse into each other to form an extended space where intimate conversation about hope and redemption between inhabitants is possible. G narrates:

> "But the season of flood could change everything. The floods could level the stature and even conceal the identity of the village... From the window I looked at the uniform wreckage of a village at night in water... Then [my mother] broke into a soft repetitive tone which rose with every fresh surge of feeling until it became a scattering peal of solicitude that soared across the night and into the neighbour's house. And the answer came back louder, better organized and more communicative, so that another neighbour responded and yet another until the voices seemed to be gathered up by a single effort and the whole village shook with song on its foundation of water..." (Lamming, *Castle* 11).

The call and response technique normally associated with the calypso in a ritual comic occasion becomes the response of a community faced with the need to overcome the psychosocial devastation caused by colonial oppression, or on a literal level, caused by the flood. The flood may succeed in redesigning the architecture and hence identity of the village, just as the colonial system may deform psychic identity, but neither of these external forces can hold back the people from establishing their own alternative mechanisms of identity construction. The singing which parades the people's overcoming in face of persistent lack and seasonal loss causes the event to become a rallying carnival metaphor, containing both acknowledgement of these powerful external forces, and the people's attempt to rise above the threats these forces pose.

While the phenomena of marketplace spectacles or spaces of carnival happenings are distinguished by the fact that they occur outside in the public spaces, the scene described above, though not literally outside, sufficiently qualifies by its structure. That is, the scene is a site of collective action by villagers, and the 'conversation' aspect of the song further strengthens the notion that it happens in a public space where several villagers are gathered.

Another of many such happenings occurs when the women, who gather this time literally outside, begin to talk about the effects of the flood. Miss Foster, in answer to a question of how she fared by Bob's mother, responds to her and G's mother: "let's go over yonder in the shade" (Lamming, *Castle* 24). We are not privy to the details of their talk, but the narrator begins a long narrative that establishes the ordinariness of this moment as well as its potential for transforming the lives of the villagers:

> "It seemed they were three pieces in a pattern which remained constant... Outside at the street corner where villagers poked wreckage from the blocked canal, it had absorbed another three, four, fourteen... Here where the fences penetrated each other and in silent collaboration produced a corner there were three. Outside where the roads crossed there were more thirteen, thirty... The three were shuffling episodes and exchanging the confidences which informed their life with meaning... Outside the others... too exchanged confidences while life flowed through them... Not three, nor thirteen, but

thirty. Perhaps three hundred. Men. Women. Children. The men at cricket. The children at hide and seek. The women laying out their starched clothes to dry... Three. Thirteen. Thirty. Three hundred..." (Lamming, *Castle* 24-25).

It is true that the narrator declares that the meaning their confidences give life to "was not clear to them. It was not their concern, and it would never be" (Lamming *Castle* 25). He even adds, "Their consciousness had never been quickened by the fact of life to which these confidences might have been a sure testimony" (25). However, we are allowed to doubt whether the narrator is to be believed on this point, especially when it is the omniscient narrator making pronouncements like this. The narrator sometimes talks in contradictions: "There was a difference and there was no difference" (Lamming, *Castle* 24). The scene previous to the gathering of the women where authority is circumvented through a series of maskings helps to mediate the assessment by the omniscient narrator that the women are not conscious of the reality of their lives.

In the previous scene, which makes even the assessments of the omniscient narrator relative and open to doubt, there is a lot of play on masking the truth. The protagonist's friend Bob comes up with a plan for each to get into a crocus bag and for Bob to pretend to be G pretending to be a 'bear'. Bob hatches this plan in order to get out of a beating by his mother whom he hopes will think that the 'bear' is really G in disguise. The beating is imminent because Bob, along with other children, has just broken down a fence between his mother's and G's mother's houses as they try to stare at G bathing naked in the yard.

It is in a similar voyeuristic desire to expose what the women talk about, that the narrator follows the women over to the shade in order to pronounce on their consciousness. However, how do we know that the narrator is not being duped, just as Bob's mother was duped by multiple levels of masking? It is doubtful that the omniscient narrator knows everything, else why would Lamming need so many narrators in this text? Narrators are G, an omniscient narrator, and instances where no narrator is present but the dialogue of characters is dramatically rendered as in a play. The destabilization of the narrative function unhinges fixed notions of the truth and meaning in a characteristic carnival move.

The carnival erasure of all boundaries is again evoked in the proposed erasure between bodies suggested in the plan by the boys to dupe the mothers and as the "[t]he two yards merged... [and] the barricade which had once protected our private secrecies... surrendered" (Lamming *Castle* 18). Bob's mother, in offering reparation for the loss of the pumpkin vine which breaks off in the confusion of the broken fence, threatens to give Bob a severe beating. Bob plays bear and the two women think it is G hidden in the bag as he passes them. Unfortunately, G's mother wants to beat him also, because he has let his naked body be exposed to view too long, so the plan nearly backfires. The narrator G says, "[My mother] took a step forward with the broken branch, and I felt my skin burn with the sting Bob would receive" (23). So it is Bob's mother who is the one who now talks G's mother out of beating G who is really Bob disguised as a bear. Through this masking Bob successfully evades the beating as the two women end up laughing at his antics.

The scene is a complex tangle of role playing and double, even triple masking—Bob playing G playing bear. That complex is indicative of carnival chaos which opens all assertions of truth to question. Thus, the narrator's assessment is suspect when he argues that even though these community gatherings happen often, the participants are unaware of their significance; the context relativises that judgement. As a consequence of all this contradiction, we need to hear the characters in their own voices to know the truth on any matter on which this narrator pronounces. The author supports us as readers in this distrust by exactly giving us scenes where characters speak with no narrator intervention.

The gathering by these women is not different from that in the shoe maker's shop where the villagers promote and give substance to the idea of the Penny Bank and Friendly Society as a scheme to buy the spots of tenantry land on which their houses are located. The villagers in the shop are fully aware that to acquire the land on which they live as tenants of the Landlord is to change historic relations between him and all he stands for and themselves. Their plan suggests that this is precisely what they want to do. It is difficult to see how as single female heads of households with direct interest in the matter of land dealings, positions which many of the women hold, they would exempt themselves from these types of political conversations. It is more than likely that in such gatherings where the women meet and do their customary talk and share "the confidences which inform their life with meaning," when the plan for the Penny Bank and Friendly Society arises, they would also participate in its promotion, along with whatever other gossips they also exchange.

Feast, Masquerade, Resistance

There is another type of carnival gathering similar to the ones described above that Lamming symbolically presents in *Castle*, and to which Burton also refers. This gathering is the tea meeting. It is an occasion that mixes singing, religious connections and food, but for Burton it is also an extension of carnival resistance.

The tea meetings were popular, regular Sunday evening activities in territories previously colonized by Britain during the early 19th to mid 20th century. Burton quotes Hill in placing their origins and development as follows:

> "Tea meetings began as church-sponsored occasions in the nineteenth century when believers met to sing hymns, eat cakes and drink tea or lemonade, from which 'inauspicious' beginning rose an elaborate variety concert with competitive items promoted by clubs and individual sponsors" (Burton 170).

At these meetings the participants sang hymns and other popular songs and engaged in 'speechifying'. The latter is a stylized ritualistic delivery of speeches which are enjoyed by speaker and audience alike more for the form and delivery and the number and length of unusual words included than for sense and substance. Indeed, if the speaker makes up these words as she/he goes along, this is fully expected as long as they are delivered with style and portentousness. The words do have value/meaning, but this is not from use as units of speech intended to deliver logical communication. Rather, their meaning resides in their capacity to amuse. Their use is therefore a constantly self-reflexive gesture that juxtaposes words, as it were, as illicit communications against certain authorised forms of speech-making and pedagogical delivery.

In this combination of sufficient words that make sense and big words made up for the occasion, speechifying scandalizes common sense and the sense of occasion associated with the Anglican sermon, the language of Shakespeare and other works of English poetry, and the legalistic delivery of the courtroom. The real value of speechifying, therefore, lies in hearing the remembered tones and seriousness of speeches as delivered by priests, schoolmasters and the judiciary, and consciously violating them with non-sense or another sense. If we bring John Fiske's analysis of other types of popular practises to bear, it helps us to understand speechifying and the tea meeting as "enjoying resistive pleasure" (182). The pleasure lies in the play of undisciplined meanings available for audience interpretation.

The issue is not so much about interpreting at all as it is about the multiplying of subject positions available for the speaker and audience to inhabit. It is also about the pleasure of creation, play and taking agency. This idea will be developed further in the chapter on "Overturning Rhetorical Modes."

Another important emphasis in the tea meeting, the emphasis on food, connects with the interest so far described on the grotesque materiality of the body as a feature of the carnivalesque. The tea meeting is so named to signal very early the fact that these occasions are also concerned with the serving of food. This concern can be interpreted as the unfolding of another dimension of oppositional play. In Barbados, where the tea meeting also goes by another name, Service of Song, that oppositional bent is evident. The singing of hymns, the delivery of apparently didactic sermon-type monologues, the fact that these events happen on Sundays, all testify to similarity with the church service. However, the desire of the participants to signify a distinct difference from the theosophical occasion is signalled both by the comical nature of the monologues, and by their inclusion of food as an important part of the occasion.

The tea meeting/Service of Song is a service only insofar as it appropriates for many the more joyous parts of the church service, the singing and audience participation. However, unlike the church service, it is very concerned to remember and feed the body. This interest signals only to make unspoken comment against the official church occasion with its Pauline injunctions against the flesh and its excessive privileging of the spiritual. The fact that the timing of the tea meeting follows the occasion of the largest meal of the week (Sunday evening meal), makes the point about the fleshy excesses of the body very clearly. The participants come having feasted only about two to three hours earlier, typically on rice and stew, fried or baked chicken, macaroni pie and assorted side dishes, and use this occasion to eat even more. According to a respondent, Lionel Haynes, whose mother used to regularly host these meetings, the typical menu at the service consisted of fried pork-chops with the rind and fat attached, fried chicken, loads of ripe bananas, sweet coconut bread, 'soft' drinks (local sodas), and 'hard' liquor (alcohol) (16-01-2005). If the time coincided with a special season, such as when corn meal conkies (type of meal pies) were being eaten in November, these would also be served.

This linking of food with the observance of religious ritual has associations with the practices of African spiritualities. Resonances of it are to be found in Haitian Vodun activities. In a section of her book entitled *Mama Lola, A Voudun Priestess in Brooklyn*, Karen McCarthy Brown concludes from her study of Vodun that, "Providing food and creating the elaborate ritual contexts in which that food is presented to the spirits constitutes the most important work Alourdes [the Vodun Priestess] does for them" (44). Brown includes pictures of the elaborate food-laden "Tables" which spirits demand and celebrants provide as ways of propitiating and accessing the help of an Iwa. She makes two significant conclusions: that food is the "major marker of the success of parties, the length of journeys, the passage of time, and of life. Few stories about important events in the near or distant past do not include catalogues of what was eaten" (43); and that "eating is more than a practical, life-sustaining activity. It is the means of identifying the in-group... And it is the means of maintaining the same group" (43).

Curwen Best directs us to a similar point about the fusion of religious and secular traditions being made by the Barbadian calypsonian, Wayne 'Poonka' Willock. Willock sings about Tuk band players who make the rounds in the neighbourhoods on Christmas 'foreday' morning in Barbados playing for food and rum. Best quotes from Willock's 1983 calypso, *Tuk Band Rhythm*:

> "Listen to de music that I bring
> Ah bottle of rum is just de ting
> Little Jesus meek and mild
> Two rum for a man and one for a child"
> (*Barbadian Popular Music* 55).

In Chapter 7 of *Castle* Lamming introduces a scene where religion, food and the celebration of the body, indicative of the Bakhtinian intertwining of high and the low, are similarly collapsed. The scene at the start of the chapter portrays an old woman with her tray full of bananas, oranges, plums and nuts. The woman is dressed in the white head tie of the women participants of a street church meeting soon to be introduced.

While she is sleeping, the small boy sitting "nestled" near her, possibly her grandson, steals first one plum which he "stuffs" in his mouth and then fills his pocket with a banana, more plums, and nuts (159).

The descent into the open body is therefore tied with transgression, and is juxtaposed with the upward movement of the white head tie and the light of the candle of the coming religious meeting. There is some ambivalence here in connection with the old woman. She is both a self-enclosed and an open body, both a sign of the downward and of the upward movement. The narrator says, "in her sleep… she was like the houses, old, weary and remote… But out of these bodies which seem lifeless there had grown others that at other times turned the air into a battle front of flashing light" (Lamming, *Castle* 159). One of these lights is the candlelight of the religious street meeting, a "flame that leapt up and down in the wind" (160). She is the one transgressed against by the system of colonialism which places her in the position of operating the informal sector activity of selling things from a tray at the roadside, even at night, in order to make her living. However, she and her progeny are the ones who also transgress. Their struggle is for an identity associated with the African-inspired Pentecostal worship in the face of orthodox dominant Anglicanism. It is also for the political and economic liberation to come with the fires of the riots foretold in the light of the candle.

The following scene describes the religious street meeting

with its combination of worshippers and spectators in terms of carnival spectacle, revellers and audience. At least for the spectators who come in their numbers to see and hear how others 'get saved' at the street church meeting, this seems to be so (Lamming, *Castle* 161). Although food is not literally present, the notion of food is still suggested in the presence of the table (one of the props of the meeting) with its white table-cloth and green bottle containing a candle. The people who come forward to be saved will be the "harvest". The boy who stands near to the worshippers who circle the table seems to be the young boy who has taken the food and run off. The women beat the cymbals as they get ready to get "in the spirit [when] they danced and shouted in a strange language [called] speaking in tongues" (161). The preacher is becoming "remarkably eloquent and he kept a special language to meet every new situation [in getting the boy saved]" (162). The captured boy and the kneeling preacher, the narrator says, "had become the spectacle for everybody's gaze" (155).

Ironically, although the preacher speaks eloquently about the soul of the boy and of the light of the "Anointed," metaphors of food and flesh with which the chapter begins still abound in the scene. For example, the text reports that the spectators, who had grown in number drawn by the singing,

> "...liked to see how others got saved, and sometimes they
> heard their testimonies which were often embarrassingly
> intimate. Their candour was a sign of their purge, and they

confessed without question the sins they had committed in thought, word and **particularly the deeds that related to the flesh...**" (emphasis added) (161).

This street meeting constitutes the camouflage of resistive intent both in terms of its restructuring of colonial religion and the fact that it serves as a refuge for the boys in a story relayed later when they breach the boundaries of the plantation and discover the lie about colonial sexuality.

The boys attempt to deflect the authorial colonial gaze by running away and hiding in the open in a street corner church meeting. By this they declare this event to be opaque to the eyes of authority, to be a mask. It is as though Lamming makes them join another masquerade band. Before, their mask was the night, but now it is a more sophisticated mask. It is Afro-Creole religion hiding out under the guise of Christianity, yet another folk masquerade from under which the folk "ambush" colonial culture. It therefore forms the perfect place for the boys to hide, in not so plain sight.

They may have difficulty with some of the interpretations of the Pentecostal religiosity, but the boys see the advantages of this collective group response to colonial cultural domination. As they seek out this mask we hear the tones of the 'speechifier' in the preacher's and the narrator's vocabulary. The boys are claiming untouchability behind the "paling* [fence] of God's

---

* paling fence

   a fence made with galvanised sheets instead of with pales or pickets

mercy" (Lamming, *Castle* 181). The preacher asks them when they pretend to make offering of themselves in order to get away to give "of the apple and peach of their days" rather than refuse the call in order to "dine and dance and wine in the sin of the flesh" (180). In addition, he warns the overseer who tries to seize the boys for their escapade at the plantation, "Touch not the Lord's anointed" (182). The author directs us to the thought that there is possibly more going on in the preacher's mind than the concern with the boys' souls.

If we examine the nature of the type of worship activity in which the boys seek refuge, it seems to be inspired more by the Trinidadian African-inspired Spiritual Baptist faith than the Barbadian Pentecostal meeting, although both share features like spirit possession which were significantly different from the practices of the orthodox Christian churches. Even though Lamming, in the taped interview, says that the latter is what he references, in the above-described scene the presence of the table and white head ties suggest that he is unconsciously transposing description of Baptist meetings he might have come across in his sojourn in Trinidad onto Pentecostal meetings which happened in Barbados. Nevertheless, both these popular church meetings distinguish themselves by their production of an identity alternative to that of the dominant culture, just as the tea meeting is different from the orthodox religious service. As a consequence of practices that were unorthodox by European standards, both tongue-speaking Pentecostals and Spiritual Baptists were ridiculed by the elite. Spiritual Baptist practices attracted even greater ostracism, as they were perceived as carnival spectacles instead of indications of 'real' spirituality.

West Indian colonial judicial systems as late as the second decade of the 20th century had no doubt about the transgressive nature of African-inspired form of religious activity. Hence, the operation of the Spiritual Baptist Church was declared as a social evil and banned by the colonial government. Marjorie Thorpe, in the introduction to Earl Lovelace's novel *The Wine of Astonishment*, which is itself about the banning and regrouping of this church, makes note of the 1917 Shouters Prohibition Ordinance passed in Trinidad (vii). Thorpe observes that in presenting this Ordinance, the Attorney General argued that Shouters' meetings made the neighbourhoods in which they were held "almost impossible for residential occupation", and that their practices were not such "as should be tolerated in a well-conducted community" (qtd. in Thorpe vii). However, as Thorpe further explains, anthropologists Melville and Frances Herskovits' investigation of the Baptist sect showed them to have reputations among the local population for probity, trustworthiness in personal dealings, and high standards of moral conduct (Thorpe vii).

The Herskovits found in the practices of the Shouters "nothing more damaging than an example of how 'African worship... had been shaped and reinterpreted to fit into the patterns of European worship'" (qtd. in Thorpe vii). It seemed that this fact, and in particular the possession phenomenon practised by the Shouters, plus the fact that the membership was black and working class, accounted for the hostility of the colonial government interested in promoting European values (viii).

Thus, by joining the group of religious street shouters, the boys in *Castle* take themselves out of danger from the private plantation coloniser, only to put themselves into another kind of danger, the danger of colonial state sanction. However, by the same token, their act also makes them more dangerous to the plantation system and colonialism as they have aggregated collectives of resistance—their own and the street Christians. Theirs is a kind of laughter which denies colonial domination. At the same time it asserts the world they conceive, of equality, freedom and abundance.

The scene ends with the worshippers (including the boys) singing, "come into my heart, Lord Jesus". Although, given the text of the song, this may look like colonialism overcoming, in another sense it suggests successful overturning of the colonial order by the danger posed by unruly Black behaviour. The boys, after all, are successful in hiding out in the meeting and the people are singing. From Trumper's and Mr. Slime's perspective, the singing of these particular words by villagers fits the metaphor of Afro-creoles stuffed with the unhealthy nastiness of colonial domination. However, by their actions the boys and the worshippers are the ones who have entered colonial space as disruptive masqueraders.

2 The Grotesque Body: Signifier of Resistance

In the face of the might and inexorable propagation of colonial and neo-colonial culture and order, historians who concentrate on exploring major political ruptures are challenged to explain why these forms of resistance emerge when they do. It is not enough to say that the folk were ready, one must ask how they got ready. Lamming's usage of popular cultural forms in his novel reveal that continuities exist in West Indian Afro-creole people's resistance to domination. These forms show that people constantly put their bodies outside disciplinary systems even as they endure them. Their use of the carnival with its specific forms is an example of how these rehearsals of resistance are staged and the discursive nature that they reveal.

The entrance of these carnival forms into post-colonial literature is an extension of that staging. This study argues for a movement in critical practice beyond the primary action of description and the pointing out of oral forms in texts to the recognition and exploration of the discourse of a little tradition. Integral to this little tradition is the grotesque body or the body which is never far from its relationship to sex, consuming and voiding, and the intense physical bodily contact of person on person violence. This body figures among the system of images that Bakhtin identifies as the carnivalesque.

Lamming also utilises images of the grotesque body in *Castle* to consolidate the critique he makes of the plantation system, colonial power and its debilitating effects, and local bourgeois institutions and values. In images of bodily consuming and voiding, sexual 'excesses' and vulgar bodily expression in general, he sets the oppressive world of colonial force, including domination by the Black bourgeois class which mimics the coloniser's culture in opposition to villagers' attempts to assert themselves against and within that system. Employing carnival play techniques and metaphors of the masquerade, he brings not just the folk as a social category, but their bodies to the text as unruly signs that seek to destabilise ruling systems and values.

However, identifying the images Lamming uses as grotesque, given that they are being associated with the lives of African-descended people, is not without danger. The stereotype of the inherently grotesque black body already exists through designation by colonialism. White colonisers and the colonial project they devised in the Caribbean needed to differentiate the black body from what is 'human' and 'good', in order to justify the expropriation of the labour of blacks under the system of maximum surplus extraction that was slavery. They, and the black and coloured middle class who succeeded them, also needed to do this as a mechanism to justify the right of the dominant group to rule.

These classes implement their projects by marking the black body as animalistic and either devoid of culture, or possessed of an inferior primitive culture that is close to the state of nature. Sylvia Wynter sees this project occurring since the 16th century with Western Europe's expansion into the New World, and calls it the "physiognomic model of racial/cultural difference". She suggests that it replaced the anatomical model of sexual difference as a way of organising social relations (357-358). Wynter sees this shift in models most powerfully enacted in Shakespeare's play *The Tempest*: "Caliban, as an incarnation of a new category of the human, that of the 'irrational' and 'savage' native is now constituted as the lack of the 'rational' Prospero and the now-capable-of-rationality Miranda, by the Otherness of his physiognomic 'monster' difference." (358) The white body, which nevertheless shares abilities to be sexual, engage in mundane bodily functions of consuming and voiding, and engage in physical contact, has been dematerialised and made subordinate to mind. The black body, though evidently capable of producing and disseminating knowledge as Caliban does about the island for Prospero, has been made to bear only its sensuous animal nature.

However, as shown by the need for the ideological work to achieve Caliban/Africa/native's designation as monster, it is also clear that elements of monstrosity can be turned inside out as in the carnival principle, to aid in affirmation of black goodness and humanity. In other words, the need to work to implement this bodily image of blacks as 'Other' suggests that an alternative image is already present and has to be suppressed.

Homi Bhabha theorises that the need for the discursive work of othering is inevitably contained within colonial power relations (32-35). Colonial power relations, Bhabha argues, generate ambivalence about the status and authority of that very power, and incur resistance to it by colonised peoples. This resistance, he argues, expresses itself through responses by the colonised of mimicry and hybridity (Bhabha, 32-35). However, the existence of hybridity brings the status of the authorising original into doubt, or raises the question of its authenticity. In this instant, hybridity asserts the historical nature of colonial and bourgeois authority against the official truth that they are timeless. As Pam Morris summarizing Bakhtin succinctly puts it, "those in authority always attempt to deny the process of time, upholding their view of things as an eternal truth. Carnival, by contrast, expresses a utopian belief in a future time in which fear and authority are vanquished." (207) A belief such as this evidently notes that fear and authority have been installed and can/ will be uninstalled. It holds this belief in the transformation of social relations to an egalitarian state as rather the natural scheme of things.

With regard to the aspect of mimicry, this too is an ambivalent sign as we saw Brathwaite arguing. On the one hand, it denotes some degree of capitulation as it gives primacy to a dominant culture, on the other it means that the coloniser is as much observed by the hybrid as she/he is the possessor of an authorising gaze. This is important because the gaze is always associated with an attempt to corral, define and explain, and is therefore always self-empowered. When the colonised is the looker, the definer, the one who corrals and gives explanation to things, at that moment she/he demonstrates her/his refusal to be excluded or contained.

Faced with the scenario just described, blacks can make several responses. They can accept and internalise the disparagement with resulting pathologies of identity. They can accept the position that what they are represents difference from European culture and standards, and rearticulate their difference as natural and good. In other words, they can attach their own meanings to difference by re/defining what it means to be human. They can also, over-reacting to Prospero and his people, repress and deny the materiality of the black body and over-emphasise its rational mental or spiritual aspects. Barbara Freedman articulates the dilemma as follows:

> "Any group previously defined by exclusion from and oppression by a social order faces the question of how to redefine itself without destroying itself. Should it celebrate the scorned values with which it has been identified, adopt the values of the prevailing order, or challenge an oppressive social structure with a more inclusive sense of difference?"
> (115)

Carnival genres exemplify my second response and Freedman's third, that is, the response which attempts redefinition. In these practices the imagination is pulled into the service of redefinition and demonstrates that in any case, the European historical project was itself masquerading its own fictions (declaration of the human as non-human) in order to control and dominate. This concern with redefinition is a concern with representation itself and so makes resistance to meaning "as meaningful in itself" (Freedman 4). If in the European colonisers' view boundaries, hierarchies, repressions, exclusions and ownership constitute his identity, then the carnival challenges these closures and returns a principle of commutability, reversals and transformation.

In the West Indies, the response of redefinition and re-articulation arises out of the alternative views on human existence that inform our hybrid cultures. This response represents an attempt to bring the influence of that other source of our hybridity (in this case, our Amerindian, African, Indian and other non-western aspects of our culture) to bear on questions of ontology. The response of redefinition in the carnival intensifies absolute difference as the grotesque body, and puts it, as it were, in the face of the dominant as a form of historical and semiotic resistance. The grotesque makes a spectacle of itself even as it accomplishes a hidden design. This is the response that Lamming makes in *Castle*, although he shows characters representing the other responses that Freedman identifies as well.

Lamming's use of the carnivalised body exemplifies the point that Michael Dash makes about the use by Caribbean literature of "corporeal imagery as an index to the process of self-formation", indeed, as a sign of "revolutionary potential" (*Lost Body* 24). Dash offers examples from Amir Cesaire and Frantz Fanon to show that in several instances their work models the ideal of revolutionary self-assertiveness through imagery of resurrected flesh. He says Fanon equates a reanimated body with the liberated voice of the revolutionary intellectual, thus: "It is a vigorous style, alive with rhythms, struck through with bursting life... The new movement gives rise to a new rhythm of life and to forgotten muscular tensions and develops the imagination" (as quoted in Dash, *Lost Body* 24).

Lamming presents this trope of the reanimated body. However, his concern is with the reclamation of all the body rather than a mere reclaimed muscularity, as Dash claims for Fanon. It seems that the concentration on the body as muscularity continues the image of the body as economic tool and thus un-liberated, which has been figured and formed by colonial principles. Bakhtin addresses this notion of the centring of the body as muscular system, associating this with the leading role attributed to the "individually characteristic and expressive parts of the body: the head, face, eyes, lips" (*Rabelais* 321). He sees this centring of the body on these parts, including the muscles, to be expressive of the new bodily canon that limits and closes the body and the meanings it can articulate. In this canon "death is only death... blows merely hurt, without assisting an act of birth" (Rabelais

321-322). This latter body represents the individual body rather than the social body of all the people.

In his case, Lamming reclaims all the body, including zones of the body that are excluded or socially ostracized, but which at the same time give the body its freedom, its protean and radical openness and slippage in Bakhtin's terms. Bakhtin suggests that the grotesque body is not defeated by death, as it operates on the boundary where one body is divided from the other. As one body offers its death the other offers birth, but the two are merged in a two-body image because of the philosophic function they perform (*Rabelais* 322). As a consequence of this openness, the body is able to produce and be representative of divergent, sometimes contradictory postures. The use of the body in this way in the text makes this form of satire multidirectional rather than binary.

Consuming/Voiding Body

Lamming sets the stage for the problematisation of the body in his representations of it in the first few pages of the book. First, he establishes the tone of raw physicality of village life in the setting with references to the "stench of raw living" (*Castle* 10). Against the traditional view of water as a purifying agent he places a view of it that explores some of its offensive but no less real effects. It can be destructive of the houses and reform the village. It can accumulate in its flow the effluent of the surfaces/ bodies that it cleans. The author draws the reader's attention to the existence of the public baths for men and women with its "perpetual stench of disinfectant pervading the air" (*Castle* 10). He further emphasises these olfactory references by directing his reader's eyes and nose to the "limestone constructions like roofless ovens for the disposal of garbage" (*Castle* 10). These limestone constructions are the equivalent of modern garbage skips and were provided by the state in Barbados in previous years for the public to store garbage until it was picked up by the sanitation authority. Indeed, they looked like traditional home-made ovens. The conjoining of images of food/bread (the oven) and garbage, expresses the cyclic continuity of life that the text explores in greater detail later.

In this first scene Lamming signals his interest in the use of the popular body as a mechanism of resistance. This interest is realised in the treatment of the body of the pet pigeon by the boy. Recalling a Barbadian ancestral wisdom that you have to 'eat well and purge clean', the boy G stuffs his pet with food (*Castle* 13). After a while, the bird can hardly swallow because the food is so much. G then instils a purge by emptying a phial of castor oil down the bird's throat. Castor oil, it should be known, is a Barbadian home remedy that parents gave to their children as a de-worming and purging agent. It was expected to produce loose bowel movements and was given just before school reopened after the long vacation in the wet season. The next morning G awakens to find the bird dead, but the narrator says nothing of the purge after this.

The meaning of this event is unexplained and ambiguous until the next reference to a bird in the text. This reference comes in the story one of the women relates of how a boy, Gordan, "the one with the chigoes", accosts a white man standing at a bus stop in the privileged section of the town (Lamming, *Castle* 20). The character of the white man as a symbol of the colonial system is rather heavy-handedly portrayed in the whiteness of the clothes and everything else he wears. However, this background of white is the canvas set up by the author on which to inscribe the stark statement of defiance the boy makes while pretending a kind of foolish innocence.

A woman reports that the boy attempts to sell the man (dressed ironically in his "white suit, hat, shirt and shoe to match") a "big, **black** fowlcock" (Lamming, *Castle* 20) (emphasis mine). Predictably the man refuses, but the boy insists and pushes the cock, turned backwards, into the former's face. The inevitable follows: the fowl messes and in its position the loose excrement covers the white man's face, his helmet and all over the front of his white suit. In the meanwhile, the other black boys come along, "the whole gang of them", and start to sing,

> "Look, look what fowlcock do,
> Look what fowlcock do to you" (21).

They clinch the act of rebellion by telling the police, who arrive after the white man has run away, that the "gentl'man mess his pants and had to run home for shame" (*Castle* 21).

The devilry, insouciance and downright rebelliousness of the boys' actions, if set against the overfeeding of the pigeon, read as an affirmation of the "death life principle" of the carnival grotesque, which Bakhtin proposes (qtd. in Morris 201). It certainly seems possible that Lamming arranges the overfeeding and then purging and death of the pigeon to exemplify just such a strategic social purging as is achieved in the scene of the fowlcock.

Lamming presents colonialism and its othering ideology as some mass congesting the people's body that needs to be released. He presents this image through a mixture of authorial intrusion and the overseer's self-hating indirect speech: "this world of the other's imagined perfection hung like a dead weight over their energy" (*Castle* 27); again in the police constable's indirect speech: "the village might have been asleep, but floating somewhere about, around, **perhaps within himself**, was the large, invisible threatening phantom, the image of the enemy. My people." (27) (emphasis added). This thing inside is like the dead body inside the living person that Pa learns about when he touches his once living friend in Panama. Pa concludes, "tis a hell of a thing, Ma, to have to live with something inside you... a next person... that you don't know" (90).

The purging of oneself of the stuff of colonialism represents life, while death is represented in the image of the white man and his associated loss of face (almost literally), and through him the loss associated with the system of domination. The

Barbadian habit of combining both the male and female sexes in the naming of the domestic bird as a 'fowlcock', lends further to this notion of bodily ambivalence and slippage.

This incident of the fowlcock is a complicated signal. No doubt the boys gain moral advantage in being able to get the better over a symbol of white domination and power. This is an instalment in the destabilisation of the dominant order that Bakhtin terms "uncrownings" (qtd. in Morris 223). Not only are the boys able to embarrass the white man, they are able to do so in a part of the town which is his domain and from which they are excluded. Furthermore, it is on the streets in public view where this incident happens and this represents another breakthrough. Other whites who dominate this area, and for who the man is a representative, could be witnesses of and hence participants in the losses incurred by this white man. The respectable street is made a carnival marketplace, and the white man is made a spectacle in this transformed space. However, it is by the black boy adopting the pose of fool that makes the scene possible. This raises questions about the cost to blacks of the act of resistance when adopting the pose of the grotesque.

It may be said that the image of the black as the fool simply reproduces one of the dominant images of blacks held by racist ideology. Whether this comic mask can simultaneously act as a figure of insurgency becomes a dilemma. It may be, though, that the act of resistance has to be evaluated in terms of what is possible for the context and time as Brathwaite's argument about the Uncle Tom strategy suggests, and as Bruce St. John supports. Furthermore, who the observer is of this act becomes critical for its interpretation. As we see, Lamming just arranges for the gang of boys to come along and not only underline its trangressive connotations with their song, but they are the ones who give the last word. They are the ones whose explanation of the scene is the one the police, as recorders of the 'truth', are forced to take since the white man is long gone, having been forced to yield ground, having been himself made into the grotesque by the children.

However, there is a second aspect of contradiction about the scene. The transformation of privatised privileged space to common marketplace in the fowlcock scene signals to us the text's significant interest in the issue of ownership of property. The relationship between the legitimate individual white man and the illegitimate gang is explored in relation to use of space. But private ownership of property is an ambivalent value in *Castle*. We are prepared by this story for the proposed change of relationship coming between the villagers and the landlord. If the villagers save enough to buy their individual lots, that relationship will change to one that is governed by modern marketplace structures and rights. They will have vested rights to their property and responsibility for its upkeep. The landlord will lose a limitless source of income and the right to direct movements of persons outside of the property he owns. However, the landlord will no longer be responsible for repairs to roads, houses or drains either. In this sense it is a necessary change, because villagers have to see that a paternalistic landlord does not serve their interests, no matter how familiar this arrangement is. It would also reveal the extent of their common interests with the workers in town, a commonality that the nature of the relationship with the landlord presently obscures. The villagers themselves see the need for the change because they invest in the Penny Bank and Friendly Society for just the purpose of securing ownership of the properties for which they have always been paying rent to the landlord.

The ambivalence around the notion of land ownership arises when one examines the reasons Mr. Slime uses to convince the villagers to save towards purchasing their lots. As Pa reveals, Mr. Slime the local ex-teacher who encourages them to buy the land, sells the idea through one argument that "tis the way the big folk think too" (Lamming, *Castle* 87). This makes the plan to own the land by the people a mimetic gesture. Mr. Slime continues his pitch, Pa says, "by giving a sort o' inside history o' some o' the nations, how they all make it they business before anything else to own the land they live on or the land nearest to them." (Lamming, *Castle* 88) This is an unfortunate argument to sell an idea to colonized peoples, if the "nations" means colonizing nations. It makes Ma's response to Pa, which otherwise looks like reactionary Christianity, appear extremely opportune and resistive: "I don't care who want land or who **take land**, the nations or anybody else, I'd only like to ask all o' them put together what they goin' to do with it", she says

(Lamming, *Castle* 88). (emphasis mine). Her question rests on the fact, as she notes, that you cannot carry it to the grave. Her idea seems the foundation for a manifesto for a land use policy that benefits those living on the land, ownership be damned.

Put this discussion together with the fowlcock story and Lamming seems to be suggesting that villagers must be able to make a complete transformation if they are to achieve true liberation. It is not enough, therefore, for the people to merely mimic the upper class residents of Belleville by themselves becoming owners of private property. In the fowlcock incident private property is made communal in the action of the boys, just as in carnival no boundaries of private ownership are respected. The villagers seem to envisage a further privatisation of the tenantry land once it is sold and broken up. In this vision the colonial model with all its problems is being reasserted. If this is the case, Lamming's ending to the novel where the majority of the villagers seem to be un-housed is not as negative as it appears. Lamming may just be opting for the more radical transformation of property relations than is generally considered. He is adopting the extreme position the carnival proposes in offering the belief that one can only transcend one's historical poverty through collective and transformative actions that return equality. Arguably, in this he may be seen as making a satirical point against the villagers—an instance where the carnival's critique is made against the masqueraders themselves. If so, the justness of his critique is open to debate.

Consider the critique of the idea of private property ownership in the context of a folksong current during the 1920s in Barbados when planters were buying up the estates formerly owned by elite absentee owners. The name of what each man has got in the song represents the name of a plantation. The words are:

> "Oh, poor me, poor me
> I ent got nabody;
> Oh, poor me, poor me
> I ent got nabody.
> Mister Gill got Pleasant Hall,
> Mister Pile got Warleigh,
> Mister Gill got Four Hill
> An I ent got nabody."
> (Marshall, McGreary and Thompson 41).

It is interesting that the composers say "nabody" rather than "nothing". If one reads it seriously, they seem to suggest, like the villagers of Creighton, that the acquisition of private property is more than adopting a pose of mimicking in post-slavery Barbados. It is actually the guarantee of a life/a body as opposed to no body. Of course, one could also read the song ironically and hear in it the critique of the state that at this time is governed by white elites who no-doubt facilitated such sales as a means of consolidating wealth in white hands. The poor African Barbadian would have had to have some body/black bodies in the House of Parliament advocating on their behalf in order to get economic democracy. In fact, in the context of the time with a limited franchise operating that disqualified most African Barbadians from voting or participating in parliamentary democracy, having such parliamentary representation would have been next to impossible.

Regardless of the translation, one recognizes that this song, as does the fowlcock carnival story, represents the commonplace resistances made by the poor. It demonstrates their insistence on taking action, often collective, but through popular cultural forms rather than through grand political ruptures to subvert if not avert systems that negatively shape their lives. They do the latter too as the riots indicate, but recognising rioting alone as a resistive act does not recognize the continuity of their struggles. Their mere survival, while not advocated as the only quality of existence worth noting, implies that balance is being wrested from attempts to dominate. To read this only as a victory of the hegemon is to devalue ordinary effort, to fail to see the value in carnival laughter, a laughter that is quite grotesque if one considers it well.

Story-telling as Grotesque Counter-production

An issue of significance in the fowlcock story related to the last point is the fact that the women disseminate the events, though pretending to be outraged. This dissemination is another aspect of the rituals of the unruly life of the grotesque body and the marketplace. It also demonstrates another aspect of the continuity of struggle described above.

The function of the dissemination of this story of the fowlcock being made to defecate on the white man is to allow others to participate in this resistive act. While the omniscient narrator tells us of the storyteller's indignation at the incident, that assessment needs to be re-examined. She obviously revels in the story and cannot wait to pass it on. The evidence for this is in her dramatization of it, which she manifestly produces for effect. It is also evidenced in the fact that though, ostensibly, she tells the story to the small group of women, she tells it in a voice loud enough for the children gathered on the fences between the houses to hear. The narrator tells us she waits while the girls on the fences titter when she gets to the part about the fowl's backside "staring in the white man's face." Presumably she waits for silence to continue her story, or rather to complete her performance. This suggests that the story-teller is achieving a certain pleasure out of the details of the story and in passing it on. She then goes on in a classic storyteller's form to repeat the statement that has just called forth a response from her audience: "Believe it or not, my child… there was the fowlcock backside in the whiteman face" (Lamming, *Castle* 20). She gets even more creative with her interpretation of how the white man takes off, not having been there to actually know how he ran off: he "pick up his heels and run like a ball of fire all the way home." (Lamming, *Castle* 21)

Despite the fact that the women are said to be indignant, they have not once reprimanded the children. Of course, after hearing this juicy story, the laughing children take off in a quest to hear more of the story and no doubt to also pass along, with their own embellishments, what they have heard. The sly narrator then tells us, "the women were left regarding each other as women sharing a common misfortune are wont to do" (Lamming, *Castle* 21). Since the misfortune is the white man's and not theirs, it is fair to suggest that the narrator speaks tongue in cheek at this moment. In other words, even the narrator becomes a participant in the ridicule.

Terry Castle's analysis, applied to the carnivalesque in eighteenth century English culture and fiction, can help to partially explain the functions in the text of the story just discussed. She suggests that the masquerade scandal threatens existing structures and moral order, and gives new kinds of status to the obscure and low (125). Such a metamorphosis occurs in the fowlcock story where all the elements of the masquerade scandal are present. Taking into consideration the other directions that the satire takes at this point, the critique it makes of the folk belief in private property, for example, we must be prepared to go beyond Terry Castle's view of the carnival to explore the way that the grotesque opens out all orthodoxies to point to real social transformation. The fact that Lamming utilises the popular cultural mode of story telling within the text at this point as the mode of plot development emphasises, to borrow an expression from Mary Russo, the redeployment or counter-production of culture, knowledge and illicit pleasures engaged in by the folk (62).

Bodily Excesses, Social Uncrownings

Lamming uses other cases of voiding of the lower body by representatives of the people to point to popular anticipation of social change.

The old woman who wanders about the streets and publicly urinates on herself breaks rules related to gender, sex, rightful place and public decency. In a context where the narrator's somewhat sardonic voice tells us that when the landlord puts out his light and goes to bed the people are expected to do the same (Lamming, *Castle* 29), the old woman is described tripping along the roadside drunk in the night with all the lights out (Lamming, *Castle* 33). And she is not alone. Joining her are hawkers of black pudding and souse, customers for the food, fornicating lovers, frogs, dogs and other symbols of chaos.

The old woman stakes claim to the night and the streets which the culture ordinarily denies to women and to the old. Her drunken state transgresses the social order in two ways: her public drunkenness suggests disorder in a general sense, but she also upsets gender role distinctions, as the drinking of alcohol to such excess is an action normally associated with men. Derek Walcott's persona in his poem *The Light of the World* voices this gender rule very clearly. Included among the folk for whom the persona in the poem has great affection are drunk women outside the rum shops who the persona describes as "the saddest of all things" (48). It is left unexplained why they should be sadder than drunken men, or than any other sad thing. The poet's description is a rather extreme view of the women's act of getting drunk, but perhaps is indicative of how threatening to all order is the woman who has not even the restraint of her own conscience or basic bodily motor control. Such is the drunken woman of Lamming's pudding and souse scene. She violates everything the landlord and his patriarchal rule orders.

Lamming goes to great lengths in exploring the grotesquerie surrounding the persona of the drunken old woman. First he connects the old woman's drunkenness and her urinating with the consumption of food. The old woman appears during the weekly sale of black pudding and souse on her once a week binge when she becomes "dead drunk". Lamming describes the food dish in sensuous detail as "a village delicacy" (*Castle* 31). It combines "the cooked intestines of the pig crammed with a potato stuffing which makes thick, heavy coils in a bowl,... [and] in another bowl the pigs ears, heels, eyes, tongue and tail [which] swim or float in a pickle of brine" (*Castle* 31). The dead pig parts shifting around in the liquid repeats the image of the old woman tottering in her soused self. It is useful to note that in Barbados to be deeply drunk is called being soused, and souse is what pig parts in the brine is called.

A second emphasis of the grotesque is in the excess of sensory detail given in the scene. The scene presents a rich collage of mixed objects, sounds, smells, actions and values. There are frogs who "whisper and wait"; a sinister fog that "conceals those who within the wood must keep awake"; the moon which "leak[s] a little on the leaves" (*Castle* 32); a young white man who makes entrance in a vehicle driven by a young dark-skinned black woman and who then joins the villagers in making their orders and does his own guzzling of the pudding and souse. There are also sights and sounds of other illicit activities going on: two dogs "bound by their hind parts... shaggy and obscene in their excitement"; and copulating couples locked and "seem[ing] as one person... gross and warm in frenzied intercourse" (Lamming *Castle* 32). Above all this, the stench of the public bath pervades the air.

> "Suddenly, the old woman totters off to the side and stoops against a tree letting her urine ooze down to the roots. Her underclothes drip, and the moon sprinkles its light on everything... The clouds move back, the light leans down, **and life oozes, a thick weight, through her congested carcass.**" (Lamming, *Castle* 33) (emphasis added)

The imagery here is suggestive of the chaos of transition, death and renewal, liberation from the status quo. The anti-bourgeois unfinished body or "carcass" of death is also the victorious community body that "guzzl[es] the pig's parts and **makes another order**" (emphasis added) (33). Is it another serving of pig's parts being ordered, or is it a demand for another social order to come into being? The tumultuous intersection of different people, animal, plant life, smell and moonlight also makes clear that the symbolism is not simply antagonistic or negative satire. Rather, it suggests that the author points toward that new order to come.

To make the last point clearer, John Clement Ball, who explores the Mennippean aspects of Bakhtin's model, makes an argument that seems to be applicable here. Ball argues: "meaning is not exhausted by [the grotesque body's] antagonistic critical representations; these may in fact be subordinate to more positive themes of regeneration and democratization" (119). I do not accept that antagonism is subordinate here, but certainly I argue that any model of analysis and interpretation must be able to account for the diverse discourses Lamming presents here.

Several codes are signalled in this scene. The crowd of villagers moves back to let the "white gentl'man" with his black female driver pass, he places his order "makes no demand, but accepts a privilege which they offer" (Lamming, *Castle* 32). Despite the suggestion that this "white gentl'man" declines to assert dominance, the code of the existing hierarchical order still exists. The fact that the villagers defer to him based on their evident belief that the white man should deserve privilege points to the existence of that code. In addition, it is signalled in the fact that he believes he should accept that deference, after all, **he does not decline to accept it**. There is also the disruptive carnival code—the fact that the white man is also a "guzzler" of the pig parts, and that his female companion with whom he disappears in the dark woods like all the other couples, is both black and his driver. His difference is folded back into the general carnival mix in which difference is a normal feature. In addition, there is the code of scandal making as a device of self-directed laughing, which is a code that also speaks of transformation. The scandal-making involves the cameo of the black woman/white man relationship.

One may argue that the black woman/white man coupling is well within the code of a status quo designed from the period of slavery, when white men took access to black women's bodies as of right because black women were presumed devoid of bodily integrity and equated with their sexuality. Some might also read it as Lamming's investment in the patriarchal aspects of that code. After all, the black "girl" may be read as being synonymous with her brazen sexuality, as driver here may also refer to her sexual forwardness. One recalls that sexual 'forwardness' or un-inhibited-ness was the stereotype of black women used by colonialists to excuse their own behaviour, and it explains why black women had such sexual harm visited on them. Some aspect of this reading is indeed present, as the narrator consistently refers to her as the "dark" "girl", while all the references to the white man speak of the "young" "man". The adjective 'dark' is meant to keep her race to the forefront and that signals some loss of her personal identity. The term 'girl' suggests an infantilisation of her and a lowering of her status relative to his. However, given that Lamming underlines and ridicules the villagers' problematic deference to him, the fact that he calls her "girl" and locates her in this historically problematic sexual liaison probably does not signal the author's intention to disparage her. Several factors suggest that another reading is also pertinent.

The first factor is that though the community seeks to recognize/define the "girl", no doubt to offer scandalous comments (as the fact that they "titter" suggests), she seems to have the author's and the night's approval. The narrator says, "There is titter, but no recognition. Her face is in harmony with the night." (Lamming, *Castle* 32) The effort to maintain the privacy of the young woman puts her and the white man in his association with her, in collusion with the night. However, it is important at this point to remember that the night is a wonderful collage of chaos, equality and transformation. In this night, urine is bodily refuse, but regains its status as revivifying water when it is symbolically viewed as seeping upward from the roots through bark and leaves. Life, in all its messiness, happens in the night —it happens outside of and in spite of the control the landlord/colonizer or the ones who try to mimic him and his class.

Life is not contained by colonialism even though that system of inequality and death congests the body politic with unwanted stuff. Instead, life persists even through the congested carcass. Life here is as Dylan Thomas (one of a circle of writers with which Lamming mixed while he lived in London) describes it in a powerful, evocative and iconoclastic image. It is the "force that through the green fuse drives the flower" (8). The complexity and riot of metaphor, especially that bound up with the natural world that characterizes Thomas' work marks this passage of *Castle* also. There is much reminiscent here too of the opening of Erna Brodber's novel *Myal* with its concern about the body of the main character, Ella. Ella's spirit is stuffed with a "grey mass of muck, [she is] choked on foreign", that leaves her lying as if dead (Brodber, *Myal* 1). A tumultuous and anthropomorphic vein also pervades Brodber's scene as the houngan or local obeah doctor calls on the forces of nature, the collective will and his imagination, to heal Ella. An analysis by Hull on the back cover of *Myal* rightly argues that Brodber uses this sense of turbulence to express her concern, to move beyond placing easy binary oppositions, towards promoting multiple alliances and democratic exchanges as the way to health for the people (back cover).

Lamming shares Brodber's concern here to explode bi-polarity and offer solutions based on difference and respect. For both of them, the **carnival grotesque** is a good metaphor through which to explore this concern, because it too speaks of excesses, intersections and jubilant life. What is also important here is the common yet unexpected nature of the responses brought to undo the life-denying work of the existing order. They are common since selected of the most democratic essences of the community—culture, nature, the imagination—but unexpected as their selection in and by the narrative process explodes old interpretations, emphases and expectations.

The second factor to help us read this scene and the white man/black woman relationship that is an integral part of it as representative of the hope of democratic transformation has to do with the fact that the young black woman is driver of the car, if one takes "driver" and the presence of the car literally. The tradition in many societies is to associate men with being controllers of technology. It would therefore have been unsurprising if the young man were the driver of the car. To have the young woman driving is a reversal of normal gender roles, especially for the times represented in the text. Furthermore, this link of black people to technology in a position of mastery also reverses a colonial norm, again especially for the times. In the context of an old problematic relationship—white black coupling—this reversal, involving agency on the black woman's part, is a way of redrawing the terms of that relationship. That Lamming chooses a black woman to be the means of redrawing those terms, and that he does not make her have to abandon this coupling as one possibility of the black woman's expression of her sexuality, is proof of his movement away from the binaries. He could after all have entertained the aesthetic choice to make the man's partner a white woman, or give the girl driver a black partner instead of a white man.

A third factor has to do with how light is used in this scene and others as a carnival metaphor for knowing and truth. The Landlord's light or perspective is not the only light there is. There is the natural light of the moon that allows the people to come out into the night and have this contrary life. The moon is very democratic, "sprinkling its light on everything" (Lamming, *Castle* 31).

In this scene the moonlight even takes on some of the grotesque characteristics of the old woman urinating in her clothes. As she enters the scene, the narrator says, "all the lights go out, leaving the moon leaking a little on the leaves" (Lamming, *Castle* 32).

In other instances the sun, another natural source, takes this position of bringing things to light/knowledge, of accentuating and synchronizing with the spectacle of the grotesque body. In the scene in the schoolyard for the queen's birthday, the sun appears brilliant, shining bright and steady "on everything" (Lamming, *Castle* 36). This natural light is contrasted with what the narrator mockingly refers to as the three "shrines of enlightenment"—the school, church and headmaster's house, which occupy the enclosed schoolyard. The author shows up the fact that these shrines are in fact failing to provide any real light. The brilliance of the sun emphasises the foul and diseased nature of what goes on in these shrines by what it reveals of the English inspector and his black understudy, the headmaster.

Given his role as education guardian, the inspector's approval of the simplistic rhyme the boys perform in the assembly in the sun presents the education system as truly grotesque. He seems satisfied to accept that what the boys perform represents the apex of their learning. However, all this performance entails is repetition of chants about how to spell 'crab' and 'go', and about the days of the months. The narrator tells us the boys had been learning these lessons for the past three months (Lamming, *Castle* 40-41)! This certainly seems to be an obscene misuse of education possibilities. In contrast, the boys in their own self-directed interpretations and learnings arrive at conclusions that suggest that to them the English inspector might represent something quite other than educational guardian. They arrive at their ideas in their discussion of how the king of England's head gets on the pennies that the school distributes on this official day.

One of the conclusions the discussion by the boys on the king's head on the penny reaches is that "the English were fond of shadows. They never did anything in the open. Everything was done in shadow, and even the king, the greatest of them, worked through his shadow… The man got lost somehow and nothing remained but the shadow" (Lamming, *Castle* 55). The sun's performance in this context is to reveal the grotesque thing; the English shadow that seeks to fill them up with their own self-hatred and the others' imagined perfection.

The subsequent brutal whipping of a boy by the head teacher for giggling during the performance is the physical equivalent of the grotesque performance that the inspector puts the boys through, and is appropriately associated with excretion, the boy's response to the beating. The beating in itself also acts as a topos of the carnivalesque, which Lamming uses several times in the novel.

The carnival ethic asserts a release from the normal restraints on physical contact between individuals, which includes administering of blows. Bakhtin identifies mock beatings as an aspect of carnival that testifies to a liberated vocabulary of gesture (Terry Castle 37). In Trinidadian carnival and in aspects of the masquerade in Barbadian equivalents, the idea of beatings is contained in the figures of some traditional masks. The character of the Pierrot in Trinidad carnival carried a whip, and according to Errol Hill, "engaged in verbal battles before exchanging blows" (91). This character disappeared around the 1920s, to be replaced by the current Midnight Robber who carries one or two guns (Hill 91). Another old time mask in Trinidad associated with beatings is the Negue Jadin. Like the stick fighters in both Trinidad and Barbados, he carried a stick. Hill informs us that "throughout the second half of the 19th century, camboulay and stick fighting dominated the masquerade" (25). Other characters that continue today to carry other weapons include the imps of the devil band who carry axes or sticks, and the military and sailor bands who carry swords and guns (Hill 93). In the Caribbean it cannot be helped but to link this expression of physical violence in the carnival with the ethic of corporal punishment that characterized both slavery and the violent responses to it.

In Barbados the traditional masquerades expressing beatings include stick fighting which was a part of traditional Crop Over festivities and the symbolic sword carried by the lead captain of the Landship. However, the notion of breaching physical contact between individuals has taken and continues to take a distinctly eroticized though perhaps no less suggestively combative turn. The suggestion of making free with the body has always been part of the culture of the carnival and the Barbadian 'wuk-up' is referenced by that ethic. Involving rotating, vibratory and percussive movements of the lower back and pelvic area, with the occasional cock of foot in the air, this dance has sufficient correspondences with the sexual act, and a particularly vigorous form of it, to scandalize conservative spectators of the Crop Over street parade. While the dance done by Landship performers is slightly more conservative, it also includes suggestive pelvic movements. Whether done alone, with a partner, or sometimes several partners at once in a sandwich of bodies, the dance captures that space between audience and dancer(s) as it focuses attention for the few intense moments of its execution on the reveller's bodies. Dancers themselves often 'grotesquely' twist their bodies to strain their gaze down at their own bodies, particularly their hips and buttocks in movement.

All the attention on this dance and the body is duly evidenced in newspaper stories and photographs after every street parade, not only in Barbados, but in many other countries of the West Indies where similar dances are done. Newspapers carry declamations against the so-called sexualized behaviour of masqueraders, and photographers have turned it into a fixed index of carnival display in the West Indies, often searching out camera angles focusing on the genital areas of masqueraders that display if not organize such images. These declamations act as though this form of dancing is not a regular aspect of any party occasion enjoyed at all times of the year in Caribbean societies, and is therefore impossible to erase from the popular culture. Furthermore, the visual possession of the performers' bodies by the criticizing audience signalled by their desire to still those bodies, keep central both the notions of individual bodily contact and uncivil bodily gestures characteristic of the carnival. The fact that this display continues despite the criticisms indicate that revellers are acting quite intentionally in this form of disobedience.

The Headmaster's action of administering the beating and the passion with which he conducts himself in doing it suggest overtones of both the carnival ritual of giving blows and the bodily contact of the sexual act. The fact that the beating arises because of a question about the queen's underwear, and it results in the boy's excreting on himself, heightens the suggestion of its sado-masochistic sexualised nature and presents it as an instalment in the system of images of the grotesque voiding body.

The beating is an act impelled by the headmaster's internalization of the ideologies of colonialism, which make him other to himself. Apparently, another boy has whispered the question during the queen's birthday performance of whether the queen's bloomers were also red, white and blue like the British flag (Lamming, *Castle* 44). Someone giggles, and this boy has the unfortunate luck of 'appearing' guilty.

The irreverent question and giggling disturb the myth-making activity of the day. Importantly, they also reveal that the boys are somewhat conscious that the event is exactly that—an occasion of myth making. The question and giggling vulgarise and domesticate the absolute standards of authority that the dead queen represents. In other words they seek to uncrown, in this case undress, her. It underlines the recognition by the boys who pose the question and those who giggle, that a masquerade is in progress with all its accoutrements of colour, flags and performances. The headmaster is therefore put under the spotlight to respond, particularly since the inspector is present during this act of disrespect. He responds after the inspector is gone with a passion that is hardly equivalent to the act. He beats the boy until the latter defecates on himself (Lamming, *Castle* 43). This foul act of beating and the resulting foul mess fit in with the descriptions the author gives of the inspector and headmaster. These descriptions associate them with disease and reference the voiding open body Bakhtin speaks about.

The inspector and head standing in the sun seem to have another presence inside them underneath their smiles. The narrator likens these presences to two cats which may sometime "spring and suck the blood of the other" (Lamming, *Castle* 40). This is a grotesque image indeed with its suggestion of cannibalism. The narrator also likens the inspector to a toe in which a chigoe has burrowed and hatched. The eggs and infection make the toe swell into a "white and shining smoothness" like the inspector's smile, "Smooth like the surface of pus" (Lamming, *Castle* 40). The headmaster on his part is described as having a "coarse... bright and black" surface, like a "bright black... leech" full of poisoned blood (Lamming, *Castle* 40). The narrator rightly identifies their condition when he describes them both as parasites.

As the head beats the boy for giggling when the queen's name is mentioned, the terror suggested in the description of him as a leech expresses itself. He has the boy bound hands and feet and stretched over a bench, held down ironically, by four of his schoolmates. The metaphor associated with the inspector of the slit infested toe releasing its burden of bad blood and pus is present in the beating, as is the image of a black leech fastened onto the body and sucking out poisoned blood. The narrator tells us that the first blow rents the boy's pants and exposes his buttocks. This causes him to let out a howl like an animal that has had its throat slit (Lamming, *Castle* 43). The head, leech-like in his continued attack on the exposed buttocks, is responsible for the body's further release of excrement. It is interesting that the boys in their interpretation of the scene afterwards suggest that it is as though the headmaster, not the boy, has something in his mind that the headmaster has to let out: "'Twasn't nat'ral the way he went about it. He sort of had you in his mind and he see there and then his chance to let you out." (Lamming, *Castle* 44). Could it be the nastiness of the shadow king's imagined perfection? For them then, the right response would be to wait till "very late at night" and stone him for his brutality (emphasis added) (Lamming, *Castle* 47). Under the camouflage of night, as under the mask, will be their time to right such "advantage-taking" by another kind of bodily grotesquerie.

The sun seems to point out the grotesque truth of the matters surrounding the education system, and it shines with a particular intensity on the headmaster and inspector as colonial representatives. Instead of the picture of secure identity as master that he and the inspector present, they are revealed as performers engaged in their own masks. The head comes in for further special attention by the author, and is revealed as a coward and a spineless figure of ridicule in all aspects of his life. After being presented as a figure of control in the schoolyard and in the classroom, the sun of truth further enlightens the reader about this opposite in his nature.

Appropriately, the additional unmasking is done via revelations from photographs, which depend on the manipulation of light and darkness to reveal and to mirror the truth of existence they propose to display. Photography is also a form of popular culture that both presents and represents (Melville 2005-07-02). In other words, it appears to speak the 'truth' as shown by its apparent transparency, but is also re-presentation of images which have been organised by the photographer. The representation implies aesthetic choice and therefore makes the photograph very much artistic (as opposed to transparently truthful) and also political. Lamming borrows from this very appropriate form for this moment to mediate an important juncture of the text.

What the light and darkness of the photograph together reveal is that the headmaster is also a victim who is being beaten literally and also by circumstances which, according to patriarchy, ought to be under his control. An envelope of pictures accidentally dropped by one of his teachers falls into his hands and exposes a grotesque truth—that the headmaster's wife is having an affair with one or more of his teachers. We learn that she also beats him at home, another grotesque truth, and that his neighbours know this. In fact, the boy whom he abuses is the son of the headmaster's maid, who also knows about the humiliating spectacle of his domestic life.

In indirect speech the head reveals the headmaster's loss of face. He sees himself as a little boy with the world "turned upside down" (Lamming, *Castle* 66). Interesting here is that the headmaster also talks about this experience as a purge. In indirect speech he ponders when he sees the pictures, "You wait with an expression of bewildering disgust for the purge of that unspeakably unwanted thing... Castor oil... Now you were sick in the stomach, and would remain sick until the purge was complete" (62-63).

The purge offers him the possibility of releasing all the poisons that he has ingested and been stuffed with by colonialism and patriarchy, including the patriarchal actions of his wife, but we do not get the idea that he will act on it. Instead, it seems as though the headmaster is also a shadow king (Lamming, *Castle* 70). He admonishes the boys in his final words to them before school is dismissed to "remember that Barbados would always be Little England... and let [that] be a feather in your caps" (Lamming, *Castle* 75). This is marked irony when we recall that the narrator accentuates this series of crises and revelations by saying, "the sun was making a new slant. It came in through the window in a straight shaft, and shot hard on the headmaster's head." (58)

The headmaster is uncrowned as clown king by the revelations of his humiliations. He is also uncrowned by the fact that the boy whom he thrashed is smiling as he disseminates the story of the head's marriage troubles, and that the boy furthers disseminates the details of this shaming by spreading the story much like the women spread the fowlcock story (Lamming, *Castle* 49).

Through the consuming and voiding, the thrashings and renewal—Bakhtin's classical uncrowning—the people are re-born (Morris 223). For though it is clear that the purge does not work in the headmaster in the sense of a radical transformation, it does give rise to a sort of perverted birth that seems for a time to hold hope for that transformation. It gives birth to Mr. Slime. The Headmaster in indirect narrative speech hints that Mr. Slime is the person whose face in the picture is hidden in his wife's lap (Lamming, *Castle* 63). After this scene Slime is no longer with the school, but is busily involved in promoting the Penny Bank and Friendly Society, and advising workers on trade union activity. These are mechanisms that can give the folk economic democracy, and the folk are willing to accept Slime's leadership in the vital changes because he is their hope as a son who has mastered the colonizers' language and systems, and who can also see value in folk institutions. As we see the unfolding of this promised transformation we recognise that Mr. Slime's character is meant to be ironic, as his name suggests. However, even in his naming, Slime, we are reminded of the imagery of the grotesque consuming and voiding body.

The Sexualised Body

Another instance where Lamming links the body to the theme of transgression of authority exists in his image of the sexualized body. Official western culture expects the body to be closed and clothed, and on a broader scale enclosed, except when the state or the system of economic production opens it to harvest the pleasures of its libidinal energies. (I take here Carl Jung's notion of the libido as the psychic analogue of physical energy (Jung 208). In this conception the instincts such as the drives for sex, hunger, power, are not individually equated to the libido, but are expressions of it.) Literature abounds with examples of European dismay/disgust/fascination at seeing aboriginal peoples wearing only their skins or insignificant embellishments (as those Europeans assumed) covering sexual organs. It is as though the visitors expect that the mere openness of the body equates with unbridled sex, hence with disruptive morality, or rather, immorality.

For the state and systems of domination, unbridled sex threatens their ability to declare order, to designate all pleasures to be productive, and to manage the production of the state's sons and daughters. In the colonial situation the forces of domination perceive these outcomes to be necessary for the stable reproduction of the colonial social order. The expectation is that sexual activity will happen within certain boundaries, sexual partners will be certifiably married, each partner will have only the other, children will have both father and mother, and orderly households will safely contain this complete triad. As the representative of this official order, the plantation household in *Castle* apparently reflects these values. Ostentatiously posing themselves to portray these values, the inhabitants of the plantation parade them in tea gatherings on the rooftop where such exhibition is clearly visible to the villagers (Lamming, *Castle* 25-28).

The plantation household also parades its bourgeois values of seemingly orderly, stable family life in the carriage-drawn rides around the village every quarter taken by the Landlord, his wife and daughter (Lamming, *Castle* 28). Importantly, the family also makes these outings after every calamity (perhaps to remind villagers of this uninterrupted subterranean order when the weather un-houses people and brings these values into doubt). The spectacular and didactic nature of these performances is underlined in the text by the boys' repetition of both the tea gathering and the carriage outing in "impressive" make-believe performance (Lamming, *Castle* 28).

Such make-believe performance by the boys is ambivalent as it expresses both the desire by villagers for the glamour such living represents, as well as makes commentary on the make-believe nature of the performance given by the plantation family. That the boys' performance makes such condemnatory commentary must be credited. We have seen already that the villagers are not above making their own interpretation of what is real and what is fictitious about the official order.

Villagers may seem to be impressed with the order of colonial sexuality; however, they live a distinctly and persistently different reality. In the text it is not just the revolt of workers in major political ruptures like the riots that threaten to destabilise the dominant order. Other circumstances in the text related to carnivalised sexuality of characters also present this threat. There are unmarried partners, children born out of wed-lock, men and women who have several partners, women who cheat on their husbands, unwed mothers who run households, boys who make play with their penises in public spaces, marriages which have gone awry or which cannot get past the wedding stage, unwed fathers whose abodes are left unaccounted for, and 'disorderly' people just generally exposing themselves illicitly. These disorderly circumstances and exposures threaten the supposed moral order of the plantation society.

Tony Tanner, quoted by Terry Castle, helps us to understand the meaning of these disorderly circumstances in the novel in general. Tanner acknowledges that the eighteenth and nineteenth century novel is a bourgeois formation, celebrating bourgeois values of marriage, social stability and "genealogical continuity" (*Castle* 115-116). However, Tanner also argues that the existence of orphans, prostitutes and adventurers in these early novels represent:

> "...a potentially disruptive or socially unstabilized energy that may threaten, directly or indirectly, the organization of society, whether by the indeterminacy of their origins, the uncertainty of the direction in which they will focus their unbonded energy, or their attitude to the ties that hold society together and that they may choose to slight or break" (quoted in Terry Castle 208).

Lamming makes these kinds of contradictions present not only among the villagers, but in his fashioning of ideal colonial sexuality itself, where illicit sexuality emerges in connection, not just with the villagers, but with the plantation and its supposed moral order (Lamming, *Castle* 177-178). In creating this scene, Lamming exposes an under-explored history of colonization which reveals illicit sexuality within the plantation house among Whites. We know from slave narratives and records like the diary of Thomas Thistlewood, a white planter in Jamaica between the periods 1750-1786, that white plantation owners and owners of slaves took the license of slavery to indulge their sexual fantasies with the enslaved (who ironically they nevertheless insisted were not human) (Hall 50). However, we do not know as much about white on white sexual misconduct. Lamming here exposes that colonial sexuality was orderly more so in the realm of ideology than in practice.

Lamming places the scene of transgression of plantation sexuality firmly also in the context of a breech of colonial order by the sexualized body of the villagers. The boys from the village are busy transgressing the space of the plantation to watch a fete in progress and we learn that this is where they have gone often to watch cats mating (*Castle* 170). If a significant principle of the carnival is to celebrate the freedom of unauthorised looking, then the boys have inserted that principle into this space of authority in two senses. They have set out to look at the landlord and his kind without permission and outside the latter's controlled performances. Furthermore, they have invaded the plantation space with a voyeuristic gaze that is contaminated with unorthodox sexuality.

Since village sexuality is associated with primordial chaos, the scene, as expected, is dark and teeming with possibilities and dangers, metaphorical life and death. The boys approach the wall surrounding the plantation with the chorus of the song from the Baptist meeting following them, "you must be born again". According to Trumper's interpretation, its images are of old age/incest/death and pregnancy, "it ain't only stupid but it sound kind o' nasty" (Lamming, *Castle* 167). The conversation shifts from a discussion about Mr. Slime and politics into a discussion about food and eating to excess. The two topics overlap on the question of the material lack of village life and the image of the open mouth centres them. Life for the villagers will be born from the imminent death or certainly the transformation of present relations with the plantation. Therefore, the death of one is pregnant with the birth of the other—images of unnatural birth of the song returns. To add to the semiotic disorder, the night is also filled with other creatures in ways again suggesting that the boundaries between one and other are indistinct.

All this emphasis on the body's natural open-ness and its absence of boundaries shifts the conversation into discussions of sex. The narrator goes into detail about the cats which assemble in the wood near the wall, "where they fight, and scream, and copulate" (Lamming, *Castle* 170). Trumper and the boys had gone at night on several occasions to watch the cats, which the narrator tells us, "mated with a kind of ferocity which fascinated and terrified the boys" (170). Trumper picks up what he thinks is a rock as defence against the possible attack of the landlord's dogs, but it turns out he has picked up two frogs which, though they drop to the ground with a thud, are not dislodged from their "hideous [mating] posture like a child making its clumsy scale over the bench" (171). As they drop, they leave a thick slime on Thumper's hand. In this thickly detailed scene where cats are mating, frogs are mating, and dogs form a menacing danger just out of sight, the boys who have broken into the property are watching and getting erotically aroused by seeing the sailors and women dancing and walking hand in hand. G says, "I was beginning to think what I would do if I had a girl nearby... As there was a God in heaven I was going to do something with a girl" (173).

As implied earlier, despite their engrossment in the scenes and sounds around them, the boys still find time to explore the meanings of what is happening and significantly, to relate these to other scenes and experiences involving expressions of sexuality. The boys wonder about whether the sailors are like the ones who can be seen in the streets, in motor cars and even on buses, who kiss up women in public, feel up their "bubbies"* and put women's bubbies in their mouths and suck on them. Trumper assures them (from what knowledge we do not know) that these sailors have better pedigree (Lamming, *Castle* 174). He then goes on to gossip about Cutsie, the black young woman who is the reason he has a key to the gate in the wall. She was to have met the overseer in the woods. The boys discuss how Cutsie's sexual proclivities are such that the only "man she ain't gone with God ain't make yet" (Lamming, *Castle* 175). However, as the boys also agree, though she is just made so, and that is her nature, "she won't give the **governor** a piece if she ain't like him" (Lamming, *Castle* 175) (emphasis added).

Despite their own sexual precocity, evidently for the boys the degree of public display of sexuality by white sailors (apparently

---

* bubbies

   creole Barbadian term for a woman's breasts

with black women) speaks of a lack of some kind, and this expresses ambivalence on their part. The street sailors seem to exist in the boys' minds in the realm of the white cockroaches of Jean Rhys' *Wide Sargasso Sea* (20). These poor whites are border creatures and signs of the rupturing of the colonial order, but the boys have not fully assimilated this and instead seem willing for the sake of the glamour they seek, to have whites remain in some pedigreed other world. On the other hand, in the reference to Cutsie's discrimination, though under scrutiny, sexuality of the villagers is defined as good, involving not only choice, but also political consciousness. This is very unlike the judgement they make of the sexuality of the white sailors or the other night creatures, which somehow they associate with a kind of terror.

The terror of white sexuality finds expression when the boys are surprised by a noise near a heap of cane trash. It turns out to be the landlord's daughter who is about to have "her first time" with a fast-talking sailor. The latter convinces her to come close so they will seem like one person and so presumably no one will know what is happening (Lamming, *Castle* 177). In this suggestion he clearly signals his experience with these things, and hence casts doubt about his pedigree. He is not after all different from those other sailors of the street, nor presumably is the landlord's daughter different from those other Black women with whom the sailors have sexual relations. Certainly, she does not in any way object to the sailor's plan.

Unfortunately for the couple, the boys are spectators of this event and can overhear their talk. Unfortunately for the boys, they disturb an ants' nest and the noise they make reveals their presence. A mad chase by the overseer and the sailor ensues, and the boys escape only by hiding in the religious street meeting. However, the sailor attempts to turn the situation to his advantage (and that of colonial 'decency') by concocting an alternative story that portrays innocence on his and the erstwhile Miranda's part.

Caught in the act of voyeuristic looking, especially on White sexuality, the boys are immediately constituted as dangerous. The 'transgressiveness' of their attempt to master through voyeurism is exposed. They pose a danger to the official order by the possibility that their unauthorised looking might have uncovered the mechanisms of ideological work. Indeed, it does uncover the guarded 'secret'—that authorized decent colonial sexuality is a performance. The boundaries must be redrawn and the rupture resealed, and the only way the colonial forces have to do this is to de-legitimise the boys' perspective before it gets out. Thus the race card is drawn; the story is quickly composed, almost without words, given the speed with which the overseer responds to the sailor's single shout: "There, there, the native boys" (Lamming, *Castle* 178). In the words of Ma told her by the landlord, "the vagabonds try to force rudeness on the landlord's daughter... She ain't thinkin' no more 'bout what going to happen than the man in the moon, an' then out come those three wicked brutes to tear her to pieces, and 'twas only the grace o' the Almighty God who let the sailor be where he wus, or they would have made a mess o' the child" (188).

Marauding Calibans have endangered Miranda's virtue, which stands here as the symbol of the order of the whole human world. One cannot help but note the beast imagery associated with the boys in the landlord's story, and hence cannot help but recognize that in this story Lamming is quite definitely referencing Shakespeare's *The Tempest* as he does later in *Pleasures of Exile* (105). Methodologically, we also have here the tradition of referencing of the 'speechifying' practice. This connection lends the text the significance of the practice, namely, the trope of Caliban's curse or transgressive revision.

Although he chooses to give his readers the story from the perspective of the compensating landlord, Lamming does so through the voice of the black matriarch Ma. Though this can be read as laughter at the normally astute Ma, more importantly, it expresses Lamming's ironic tone of laughter at the expense of the colonial system. He reveals the landlord to be not much different from the women or the boys who spread the fowlcock story. That is, he is someone who needs to work to propel the image of himself he selects.

Like Prospero, Mr. Creighton presents himself as the decision-maker and arbiter for his household and the village. His women, his wife and daughter, are important to him in so far as they anchor his image as ruling patriarch. However, here,

Lamming cracks the image to demonstrate the white woman resisting patriarchal domination. This is presented both in the image of the chronically ill mother (the mad woman in the attic according to Jean Rhys' *Wide Sargasso Sea*), and the daughter who stages the attempt to take control of her own sexuality.

Lamming turns away from the traditional masculinist solution to the dilemma he creates here, and in this he shows up Shakespeare's choices as in fact sexist and racist. Unlike Shakespeare, Lamming gives the white woman subjectivity and agency not only vis-à-vis the black man, but also vis-à-vis the patriarch. Ideologically, the fair/white female body was not to be publicly exposed. It was especially forbidden to blacks, but even in respect of the woman herself, her body was alienated as a site of her own pleasure. Evidently in *Tempest* Miranda faces such a problem given to her by Shakespeare. However, here Mr. Creighton's story of the reported rape is shown to be exactly that, a story trumped up by the real culprits, the predatory white sailor and the white, not-so-chaste Ms. Creighton. Her silence about the truth of the attempted rape both establishes her culpability as well as seals her 'guilt'. If the boys are Caliban as per Mr. Creighton's story, Lamming insists that it is Ms. Creighton who is likely to people the isle with little sailors, not Calibans.

Lamming also takes the un-Shakespearean move of making the black 'Caliban' desire other than the white woman, satisfying a critique of Shakespeare's *Tempest* brought by Sylvia Wynter

(355-372). G is aroused seeing the sailors and young white women dancing together, but what he wants is a local girl, not one of the white girls, although to do what with he is not quite sure. This is also suggested by the story the boys have told earlier about Cutsie, whom they seem not only to admire but to desire despite their undercutting derision of her. So, while for Shakespeare there is no woman for Caliban other than the iconic white woman, for Lamming there is always the black Cutsie. Despite saying this, one should note that Cutsie is her own woman and not that of any Caliban. She may be criticised for being free with her sexual favours, but she is emphatically not a pimper's paradise (a pimp's whore whom he sells), neither for the colonial man nor even in the sense of being Caliban's property as Wynter's "Caliban's woman" concept unfortunately suggests (355).

As we have said, Cutsie is the one who has given the key to the plantation grounds to the boys, though these grounds constitute a space that the overseer manages on behalf of the plantation owner and from which he would on the owner's behalf exclude the boys. By giving them the key, Cutsie indicates that she makes independent and contrary decisions even against any Caliban—the overseer who had given her the key so they could meet for illicit sexual purposes—anyhow.

Lamming reveals the whole world as indeed human, not least Miranda who loses symbolic status to become an ordinary girl with 'bubbies' and other sexual machinery in the context of the boy's alternative knowledge of her and the sailor. In this world of human equality all sides are shown adopting masks in an effort to save face and ensure control. We cannot assume that the landlord's version of the sex scandal or Ma's will hold sway over the version the boys are sure to spread, given the love of scandal existing in the village. Truth has been relativized and it has been made so through a series of scenarios and images involving the sexual body.

Violent Bodies

It was earlier established that violent person on person contact is a significant aspect of the imagery surrounding the grotesque body. I want here to develop that idea in more detail and widen the theoretical context for understanding it.

One of the features of carnival that is an integral part of West Indian carnival activities historically is violence that is directed by participants at each other. The stick fighting activities that existed as part of the display of festival activities, when coupled with the competition of carnival bands for street space and prominence before the judges, have led to violent confrontations at carnival time in Trinidad. The research has not yet emerged about this kind of violence among revellers in traditional Crop Over or Landship activities, but one cannot take for granted that festival activities in Barbados were without incident. Gordon Rohlehr gives an interesting history of a band of Barbadian immigrants to Trinidad who formed a band called Newgate. This carnival band is said to have disrupted the carnival activities of 1883 of that country. (*Calypso and Society* 28) Apparently, the Barbadian band was particularly "interested", Rohlehr tells us, in beating up French-speaking bands. This suggests that Barbadian revellers were not exempt from this type of violence directed by groups of participants against each other.

Rohlehr accredits this inter-group fighting to the results of displacement, urbanization, poverty, and status conflicts among contending ethnicities (*Calypso and Society* 52). However, this hardly explains the significant degree of man/woman fighting and the fighting that took place within sexes, in rural areas, and outside of the carnival activity. Following Fanon, the explanation for this violence is placed within the context of the coercive nature of official culture and in this case, colonialism. Fanon says:

> "The symbols of social order- the police, the bugle- calls in the barracks, military parades and the waving flags- are at one and the same time inhibitory and stimulating; for they do not convey the message 'Don't dare to budge'; rather, they cry out 'Get ready to attack.'... The settler's hauteur and the settler's anxiety to test the strength of the colonial system would remind him at every turn that the great show-down cannot be put off indefinitely" (41).

The constant threat of violence against the person by the colonial state necessarily permeated into popular culture and this displaced violence found its outlet among the populace. The portrayal of this violence in Lamming's *Castle* follows a narrative strategy in certain kinds of writing in Barbados that pre-dates him, and that other writers take up since him.

The *Lizzie and Joe* dialogue series written in stylized Barbadian Creole in the newspaper during the late nineteenth century is one example of a local narrative piece that portrays, among other things, the endemic violence among persons. This narrative was written by Edward Cordle for the *Bridgetown Weekly Recorder* and after Cordle died, was written by Archie C. Greaves for the *Herald Newspaper* (Forde 37). The narrative is structured on conversations between two women where one, Lizzie, tells the other, Sue, about her life with her spouse Joe, and shares her opinion about the issues of the day. Curwen Best feels that this narrative stereotypes working class black persons, although he does not explore why the specific stereotype relating to violence should arise (*Popular/Folk/Creative Arts* 241). In the following excerpt Lizzie is planning for a woman who hopes to rival her for Joe's affection:

> "But when she tink she gwine see Joe,
> she gwine see me face,
> when a put my big hand pon she,
> and drag she ouk the place
> she gwine tink a donkey kick she
> and wish that she was ded
> a gwine gie she all the butting
> a got ouk side muh hed." (Cordle 12)

Barbadian writer Jeanette Layne-Clarke focuses much of her performance pieces on person-on-person violence. She scripted an entire comedy revue called *Pampalam* that is precisely on this theme. *Pampalam* is a creole word meaning "any bothersome row or disorderly proceeding" according to the Richard Allsopp *Dictionary of Caribbean English Usage*. Allsopp also links the etymology of this word to the Twi word 'pam' meaning the report of a gun, and the Fante word for 'to persecute' (425). In the book, *Pampalam Inside De Place*, violence is the norm: three women, Gladys, Dinks and Vicey fight over the man Rannie Browne (3); Ina Birch beats up the preacher Pastor Broome for "filling her niece head with vice" while conducting sexual relations with other young women in the village (10-11); the homosexual, Punkey Malone, and three women beat up another group of women during a political meeting (41-43); Tootsie, another homosexual, along with several women, beat up on an Italian chef in a local restaurant (77); and so on.

In a manner that recalls the fights in the *Lizzie and Joe* and *Pampalam* narratives above, several fights occur in *Castle* that are either reported or played out directly almost every ten or so pages. The fights are sometimes only verbal as when G's mother curses off the sanitary inspector for checking her water barrel for larvae (Lamming, *Castle* 14); or when Susie threatens to poison out Jon's guts if he marries Jen and not her (123); or again when the shoemaker curses off the sanitary inspector who comes to evict him after Slime clandestinely sells off the land (234-235). However, fights are often also very physical.

Several of the physical fights occur over romantic relationship problems. Two villagers, Sheila and Baby, fight on one occasion when villagers are gathered by the bread cart (Lamming, *Castle* 104). The fight starts because the women disagree over the gossip about the number of months pregnant a young woman is. Bambi beats up his two women, Bambina and Bots (Lamming, *Castle* 137-138). Bots and Bambina fight over the accusation of responsibility for Bambi's changed behaviour (138). The two women fight over who will be responsible for burying his body. The undertakers whom each woman hires also end up fighting over the body (138-141).

The violence could also be quite symbolic as in the scene when the boys place pins (the older boys place nails) on the train track to make blades (Lamming, *Castle* 31). The train is set up metaphorically like the system of authority, which is threatened by this action. It is said that using nails like the big boys use can derail the train. In addition, among other uses, the bigger boys use their blades to threaten the small boys. The scene ends with a sense of foreboding: "The small boys were... jealous. It would be a long time... before they could brandish big blades" (31). Then, there is the occasion of the riots (189-208) when the violence coalesces.

Lamming presents the violence in the text in the sense in which historian David Browne describes the actual 1937 events, that is, as a long-term struggle which finally erupts as a social response to oppression. Browne, writing of the 1937 disturbances around which Lamming models his riots in *Castle*, argues for these events to be considered a rebellion "of the most profound form of political protest" (150). He argues that the term 'riot' suggests "any unplanned interruption of tranquillity by a mindless mass of people with no highly developed political consciousness" (150). Instead, he posits, these "disturbances were the highest manifestation of **a protracted struggle** of oppressed people to achieve civic rights, freedom and justice" (emphasis added) (149).

Lamming directly substantiates the argument that Fanon uses that much of the person on person violence is displaced violence or avoidance. Fanon argues, "It is as if plunging into a fraternal blood-bath allowed them to ignore the obstacle, and to put off till later the choice, nevertheless inevitable, which opens up the question of armed resistance to colonialism" (42). Lamming has his narrator reflect on this auto-destruction in his talk on the image of the enemy my people:

> "And an enemy was to be destroyed or placated. The landlord's complaint [about the stealing from the plantation] heightened the image, gave it an edge that cut sharp and deep through every layer of the land. And this image by continued assertion had become a myth which like rumour drifted far beyond the village..." (*Castle* 26).

Again, in the narration of the bread cart fight, the narrator says, "that was the way of villagers. They had no patience with choosing the right moment for anything. An assault on their daily bread or life itself just happened." (Lamming, *Castle* 104) The re-emergence of the bread cart during the riots and the linking with these events of Mr. Slime as a leader supports the idea of protracted struggle. They lend credence to the idea that the person-on-person fights are a kind of rehearsal for the riots. The rioters overturned the carts that were making deliveries and either ate the loaves or used them as weapons to throw at the police (200). Mr. Slime, who is involved with the savings society, also helps with the peoples' struggles to create a trade union movement and hence, with the riots. These links suggest that we are to read the other occasions of violence as connected to the fight against colonialism in the way that Fanon suggests and in the way that Richard Burton also suggests with his notion of a carnival continuum.

3 Overturning Official Rhetorical Modes: The Oral Text/ Creole Narrative

When Lamming asserts that peasants and the working class were shown to have the capacity for history when they were put in the West Indian novel, even he did not recognise the ways they already made this apparent even before the novel. Their vernacular forms already self-consciously pointed to the capacity for subjectivity, and hence history. By taking into the novel *Castle* the play of invention and distancing that the masquerade and its speech forms involves, the writer makes strange the English book. In this sense, Lamming uses the black metaphysics of the street to authenticate the English/West Indian book. Lamming chooses to write about the people's emergence in his book rather than the politician's life and times. In doing so, his text becomes an utterance of the people. It is an utterance for which their carnivals had long been a rehearsal and a gathering.

Lamming's stated purpose in exploring the theme of colonial experience, as he explains in *Pleasures of Exile,* is to make "a calculated challenge to that habitual way of seeing that has become a normal part of colonisation" (157). One of the ways he undertakes this alternative emancipatory task in *Castle* is in his contribution to the liberation of language and the oral culture. As is well established now, under colonial domination language is bound up with the formal education system, and is calculated to perpetuate colonial rule. It also functions to value the culture of the colonizer over that of the colonised. Critical assumptions of this attempt to impose a standard language hold that roles, univocal and hierarchical, should be understood and easily performed, and all linguistic practice should observe boundaries of space and occasion. Further, the standardisation intends that meaning should be closed with no uncomfortable personal decisions having to be made that generate ambivalence.

The outcome of the organisation of the colonial regime in language is that many experiences of the colonized are marginalized, particularly when it comes to expression of these in written texts. Lamming challenges all these prescriptions both in terms of his own language practices in *Castle*, and in terms of what he reveals inside the novel of the folk forms and folk responses operating in the society outside of it. Lamming's language practices and the ones he represents constitute what can be regarded as creole narrative.

Creole Narrative

This study goes beyond using the conventional term creole alone in describing linguistic practice, as in this usage it appears to be limited in meaning to the vernacular. Creole in this study includes but is not limited to a particular local spoken vernacular, which in any case is limited in *Castle*. Rather, it refers to a whole rhetorical and perceptual mode that includes performance, attitudes by the subject to his/her context and to him/herself in that context. It also refers to the material culture which operates at the level of language to produce and communicate meaning. In other words, it describes truly total expression.

In describing the characteristics of his concept nation language, Brathwaite notes that this language comes from the oral tradition, and consequently is part of what he calls a total expression. He observes that the oral tradition relies on a call and response mode, where speaker and audience are joined in community that is needed for meaning to be settled:

> "Hence we have the creation of a continuum where meaning truly resides. And this total expression comes about because people be in the open air, because people live in conditions of poverty ('unhouselled') because they come from a historical experience where they had to rely on their breath rather than on paraphernalia like books and museums and machines. They had to depend on immanence, the power within themselves, rather than the technology outside themselves..." (qtd. in Ashcroft, Griffiths and Tiffin 312).

Brathwaite's conception of "total expression" is a significant advance on understanding the creole linguistic milieu. However, in the context of the definition of creole narrative outlined earlier, Brathwaite's statement that the oral tradition did not utilise technology outside the bodies of the people would have to be identified as problematic. As Brathwaite well knows, people occupying that oral world he describes transformed both found and other objects like the conch shell and bamboo, cow bells and parts of plantation machineries to create technologies that helped and continue to help them convey a variety of messages and meanings not sanctioned by the dominating systems. This is well borne out by the various evolutions of the drum when this was banned for its resistive linguistic role. A spectacular example of this is the creation by the working class in Trinidadian society of a musical instrument, the steel pan, out of empty oil drums. As explored further in the section of this study on calypso, drums and these other technologies were used to send messages that advanced rebellions. Lamming's use of creole narrative in *Castle* extends this tradition, but in ways that canonical readings of that text have yet to fully imagine.

To help us explore this new way to read *Castle*, we turn again to Bakhtin. The use of creole narrative in *Castle* performs in some aspects the functions Bakhtin identifies that carnival speech forms carry out. Bakhtin identifies two such forms in European Renaissance and Middle Ages.

1.   Comic verbal compositions: the parodies, both oral and

> written which were parodies of learned treatises and even
> of Christian scriptures.
>
> 2.   Various genres of billingsgate: abusive language,
>   profanities and oaths, and other patterns of speech such
>   as indecent expressions (qtd. in Morris 196).

For Bakhtin these languages of the marketplace express carnival familiarity, and are opposed to official and serious speech because they are based on laughter (qtd. in Bahktin Reader, Morris 197). This language, Bakhtin says, "built a second world and a second life outside officialdom, a world in which all medieval people participated more or less, in which they lived during a given time of the year" (qtd. in Morris 97). He asserts, "To ignore or to underestimate the laughing people of the Middle Ages also distorts the picture of European culture's historic development" (qtd. in Morris 197). Creole narrative, although not only dedicated to laughter or limited to a given time of year, functions in this alternative sense to colonial culture and language. It has two forms in *Castle*:

1.   Performance/double talk
2.   Gossip/reliable rumour

Just as creole narrative redesigns, redefines and adapts speech performances in order to liberate spaces for use of those excluded from social power and benefits, so Lamming takes the form that is expected to show moral and emotional development of a young man coming to adulthood, and redesigns, redefines and adapts it to represent the lives of colonised West Indians.

The characters may, or may not, show moral and emotional development by the end of the novel. In his redesigning he pulls several genre forms of literature—novel, play, diary, poetry—into this novel in a characteristic creole move. Whatever the motivations for such a move, the emergent form expresses ambivalence about the great tradition. It reveals an attitude to the tradition which is at once attraction and negation. In this misuse Lamming draws on the language of the oral world and its comic spirit to effect their reversals and inversions. Eddie Baugh notices this comic twist in other West Indian writers and argues that it may even be taken as "one characteristic feature of West Indian writing" (7). This twist also exists in *Castle*.

Double Talk

As argued, Lamming entered an aesthetic whose lines do not begin or end with the 'literary' text, but which includes 'texts' not normally thought of in the same breath as *Castle*. As mentioned earlier, these include popular comedy pieces like the *Lizzie and Joe* series and the works of Jeanette Layne-Clarke. Layne-Clarke's work includes *Bajan Badinage* and *More Bajan Badinage* which are published collections of performance monologues; *Pampalam*, a drama production in which the monologues first appeared on Barbadian stage every year for the last 29 years; and "Lick Mout Lou", a newspaper column presented as a letter in the Barbadian vernacular—Bajan—by a fictitious woman called Lou to her fictitious Barbadian friend, Nesta, in England. One can immediately note Layne-Clarke's use of Cordle's strategy in *Lizzie and Joe* of presenting his text as a conversation between two women.

Curwen Best has argued that Cordle did not "project [these characters] as a means of serious expression" (qtd in Howe 240). However, the context of the publications questions this conclusion. Cordle uses creole as his medium in a press that ordinarily utilised only Barbados Standard English. Despite its publication of this letter, such a press would not, in fact, even have considered that it was giving authority to any but the king's Standard English. That press set off Cordle's pieces by the way they arranged them to be separate in terms of their relationship to surrounding columns. By so doing, the newspaper would have attempted to 'other' this presentation even as it re/presented it. However, the presence of this creole enactment immediately signals a world in dialogue, as Bakhtin would say. This signal automatically draws the politics of linguistic struggle onto the table, whether Cordle intended his pieces to be serious or not. They become serious even while being 'playful' in this context.

Evidence from their form as well as contents suggests that Edward Cordle sought through his pieces to offer a social critique of Barbadian folk manners, and indirectly, Barbadian and English politics of the time. The characters are rendered as stylised portraitures, giving Cordle the flexibility to range across and expand the boundaries of actual Bajan vernacular forms. In this way, he could create viable characters able to represent aspects of Bajan spoken in ways that would resonate as familiar speech acts, and hence get the attention of readers of the newspaper. Furthermore, he could also utilise speech genres of English artistic literature such as irony, caricature, punning, allusions, double speaking and the like, to achieve political mileage.

A letter published on January 13, 1877 in *The Times* newspaper, a paper of the coloured middle-class in Barbados (Janina Fenigsen 73-74), suggests something about the maturity of the tradition in Barbados that Lamming extends. This letter demonstrates, as do the Layne-Clarke and Cordle pieces, several of the features of creole narrative.

The letter was purported to have come from a teacher and was written in the representation that is associated with creole 'writing'. For example, it includes words that signal their difference from Standard English by non-standard spelling, it uses the apostrophe to signal sounds of Standard English that are missing; it makes-up or misuses portentous-sounding words; its themes include reference to physical violence. The full text of that letter, represented below as it appears in Janina Fenigsen's article, becomes important for this discussion.

> "Sir, - I embrace this opportunity of writin' you dese few lines, hopin' when it comes to han' an' it will fine you, an' all fambly in a perfec' state of salabrity as it leaves me at present.
>
> My name is not Peter Hog Head, but I let you know that I intermission with my godfathers, and my godmothers,

whichin is Master Sammy Manderson, an Mister Isaac Grant, whichin is parental to a feminine mother of Master Grant. So look not on me because I am black, but of intellectuality, an larnin' as yourself, an' will take out a summons for any nickname of a gentleman.

Hopin' you are in a state of salabrity, and best love to all fambly, whichin as it leaves me at present with possession of C-1-e-a-v-e leave to split your mout if you interfere wid your superior of intellectuality.

I am, Sir,
Your most 'bejent servant
PETER HEMMINGS" (qtd. in Fenigsen 73-74).

The textualization of this material and radical reality that is creole becomes significant. Normally, state and official socio-political structures attempt to marginalize this reality at best, and at worst deny it existence. Being fully aware of this, the writers who use this form nevertheless adopt this creole narrative for print. This form uses songs, storytelling, performance speaking, creole languages and oral modes to represent in the face of such domination and rejection. Therefore, its presence in print speaks of the success of creole as a counter culture.

One scene Lamming produces in *Castle* uses the headmaster to demonstrate the exclusion and diminution with which the colonial system treated creole culture. However, a careful reading of the narrator also reveals a conflicted but nevertheless insurgent spirit of autonomous self-creation through creole narrative.

The headmaster demonstrates the rule of colonial orders into which he is almost fully integrated after he intercepts the envelope of pictures of his wife and a teacher in a clear statement of sexual misconduct. Lamming effects distancing of the headmaster from himself by having the narrator give us access to his thoughts while the head appears particularly void of initiative, creativity or even passion. This and the nature of the thoughts themselves, reveal the extent of the head's subordination: The narrator says, "Formerly he had the ready response, the manufactured word or phrase and the cultivated face. He had always had these for any occasion." (Lamming, *Castle* 66). Even his final response, which calls for decision-making on his part in this very personal matter, shows the degree to which the headmaster is spoken rather than speaks his own story. This response is couched in terms of a patterned reaction that leaves the structure of power intact: "Whatever he did, he had to remember what his duty was" (Lamming, *Castle* 67).

We recognise that the villagers have some part in what the head teacher might be expected to do in such a circumstance. The narrator says, "if he failed to live up to their expectations he would immediately become one of them" (Lamming, *Castle* 67). Self-hatred promoted by colonialism has greatly shaped this understanding that simply being one of them would imply some sort of a fall. Nevertheless, paradoxically, the narrator also tells us that they respected him because "he was one of them who knew their ways. A poor boy who had done well...

He satisfied the authorities, and he had won the villagers' admiration" (Lamming, *Castle* 67). We also learn: "They respected in the highest degree everything that they violated"; and "He had to live in a way which they admired and respected **but did not greatly care to follow**" (Lamming, *Castle* 67) (emphasis added).

If we are to believe these comments but note the contradictions they express, then it appears that the villagers constitute their identities more in the breaking of the rules than in corresponding with the identities which the system of colonialism has prepared for them. While the disciplinary gaze of the coloniser hovers indirectly in the headmaster's understanding of his role and his duty, so too does some ideological authority that is represented by the villagers themselves. Apparently, other ways of assigning meaning and the ascription of other meanings to phenomena held in common by villagers and the higher orders exist.

The photographs and their appearance symbolize the very antithesis of duty, obedience and respect for authority. As a semiotic device they signal rebelliousness on many levels. There is the obvious dereliction of gender duty which the headmaster's wife displays. This is compounded by the sexual disobedience she obviously practices in both engaging in extra-marital alliances and in allowing them to be re-enacted in the continuous public text of the photograph. Whether publicly exhibited or not, unless destroyed, the photograph exists as a possibility of viewing by other than the persons involved in its intimate production. She evidently has little care about this. Further, the person in the photograph who is hiding his face is the man whose head is buried in her lap. She, on the other hand, clearly exhibits her identity in this disobedient act for the voyeuristic photographer and any other viewer.

In addition, there is the abandonment of filial respect of the subordinate male teacher for his headmaster. In an Oedipal turn the teacher blinds his head/father with the evidence of sexual misconduct with the mother, and leaves the father floundering and unable to recover his life of respect and authority. Or in Anancy style, suggested by the bizarre way the intelligence comes to hand by serendipitously falling out of the teacher's possession, the outrageous Anancy/teacher pulls a big trick over the self-styled authority figure. True to Anancy fortune, the deception is ultimately discovered. Then again, true to Anancy fortune, the culprit is not quite defeated as it is never settled who exactly the man was. Even if the trickster is the Mr. Slime who is later severed from the school, that Mr. Slime, like Anancy, manages to survive with aplomb.

There is a further way this event spells of insubordination. The photograph as a form of representation located in popular culture is itself a contested site, traditionally being subordinated to the earlier established discipline of fine arts as a form of visual representation. A growing scholarship on this form discounts the very basis on which such subordination has flourished. The traditional assumption is that the photograph represents some form of realistic/unimaginative truth that has been revealed by help of technology, more than it represents embodied creative skill (Leigh Binford n.p.). With this history in mind, the use of this subordinated form in the *Castle* scene can be interpreted as a further way the people challenge established Truth through a creole bastard form, the photograph. The headmaster's handle on Truth has been disturbed. "Everything was simple till he saw the photographs. Teaching, eating, loving, hating. He did them all by a kind of habit. Now he had to decide. He had to do something, and he didn't know what it was" (Lamming, *Castle* 67).

Lamming even more dramatically presents this challenge by creole narrative in another aspect of the scene where silence represents the will of officialdom and noise is the people's counter-production. Lamming signals the desire of colonialism to silence the colonized by enforcement of norms and refusal of individual power to interpret in the way he makes the headmaster attempt to establish discipline in the school through use of a whistle. The narrator tells us that both teachers and pupils have come like animals to understand the headmaster's wishes without his having to resort to language, as he makes different sounds on a whistle to get their attention (Lamming, *Castle* 55). They collectively and faultlessly interpret the gestures and sounds he makes using his whistle. However, in this single-voice realm and willed silence, the colonised nevertheless voice their boisterousness and capacity to disobey. The mere fact that the headmaster has to bring them to attention and resort to beatings when the whistle is insufficient suggests that he does encounter boisterous disobedience. The case of the boy's comment about the queen's bloomers which is part of this scene and the laughter that it invokes is a prime example of this. Then in a kind of moral victory by the challengers of Truth, after the photograph, the head's old authoritarian self appears defeated. "He blew his whistle and silence was present like a man taking an authoritative look round the room. As quickly it was gone" (Lamming, *Castle* 70).

Explaining My 'Explanitories'

Some elaboration is required to support the claim that much of what Lamming does in structuring *Castle*, Cordle's *Lizzie and Joe* series and Jeanette Layne-Clarke's works all share a common ancestry which the 1887 letter exemplifies. The claim about this connection might be rejected by many because of how these other texts have been received relative to *Castle*. While Lamming's text has been claimed as canonical West Indian literature and adopted into academia, the dialect performance works fail to attract the attention of the education system at any level. Only very recently has Layne-Clarke's work made an appearance in academic critical work by Curwen Best. Only Best gives this critical hearing to the work, which is surprising considering how long Layne-Clarke has been producing and how popular the work is locally. In structure and local impact, it is not dissimilar to that of Jamaican Louise Bennett, whose work is in the literature curriculum of the UWI Jamaica campus. There is therefore slim established critical authority for my argument here. This poses me in the position of having, as the title of this subsection says, to explain my 'explanitories'. 'Explanitories' is a Bajan creole word meaning observations offered in laying out an argument. It is the kind of made-up word that would have been used in speechifying at Service of Songs or Tea Meetings. It stands on self-authorisation as its ground for existence.

I recognise the apparent irony (some might say error) in my use of the *Times* letter of 1877 to represent the struggle against linguistic domination. It may seem particularly ironic that I use this letter as my context for discussion of use of the creole voice as a sign of linguistic struggle and as a challenge to marginalisation and domination; and that I do not use it rather as a sign of continued marginalisation of the creole voice or of maintenance of linguistic hierarchies. Perceiving it in this negative way might be expected, for it would fit the usual claims about creole pieces which have been created by members of the middle class (Fenigsen 74).

The contents and form of this letter (created by a middle-class writer), it would be argued, suggest that it deliberately appears to parody the oral voice and hence, on that ground alone, would disqualify as a transformative or counter-cultural strategy. As Fenigsen rightly points out, its deliberate and concentrated use of pseudo-phonological spelling, use of the apostrophe to point to the absent sounds of Barbadian Standard English (BSE) and especially its use of malapropisms, are contrary to the writing practice of creole speakers who are "trained in and committed to BSE (Barbadian Standard English) Literacy" (74). As such, the letter may be read as an attempt to parody creole language; hence, it could be seen as reactionary, or at the least as complicit in maintaining certain class and race distinctions. However, this kind of critique that Fenigsen and others make takes too literal a reading of this form of creole writing. Even if they read it as fictional literature, the conclusions above would suggest that they are reading it only in the vein of literary realism. These readings fail to take account of the self-conscious address of irony and play that marks the tone of the piece.

Two features support a case of reading this piece as ironic and drawing on the strengths of deliberate playfulness: the deliberate inclusion in the *Times* letter of both formal and sophisticated phrases of Standard English ("I embrace this opportunity"); and Bajan creole phrases ("whichin as it leaves me at present"). Such integration is an important part of the politics of the creole narrative voice. Its inclusion of both elaborate and deferential salutations, along with a threat to verbally abuse (to 'buse' as we say in Bajan) the person who is being saluted, is another example of this playfulness. This is an incongruity that can only be artistic in intent. The writer says: "hoping you are in a state of salabrity and all fambly" and follows this with "with possession of C-l-e-a-v-e leave to split your mout if you interfere wid your superior of intellectuality." Apart from the incongruity of writing a letter which at once pays honour to and curses off the recipient, this address is deliberately coining words as it goes along. Such a move is quite deliberately and quite self-consciously ironic.

Here the expression, the display or flaunting of the power to choose to be both formal and self-consciously self-authorised in using creole narrative, or 'own-way' as we say in Bajan, is a characteristic of the language the writer appropriates—the creole narrative. Kamau Brathwaite is a master of this type of 'own-wayness' as his whole oeuvre charted in what he calls "Nation Language", demonstrates. English, or the "grander narrative of progress" as Bhabha calls it, is instituted as "demotic" by the insertion of this language. (Homi Bhabha, *Culture* 246).

The writer of the letter, whom I hypothesise as coloured or even local white (because of his profession in the period) could well have been choosing the dialect precisely because it flaunts this resistance to authority and domination. I suggest he might have been seeking to make his own stabs at a colonial authority that would have also circumscribed his ability as a local to manoeuvre, and arguably, might have used a form that all well know takes this oppositional stance. Such language would achieve two ends, that he is heard and that he is overheard. This notion of being overheard will be discussed in more detail in examining Layne-Clarke's work, but it speaks to the fact that the language aims to convey more than it says.

The writer of the letter is well aware of the 'denigrated' status of the Bajan creole as his heavily satirical phrase "superior of intellectuality" shows, and is using this medium to be witty at the expense of the Standard English interlocutor. The latter's voice is paradoxically returned through the creole. In other words, the letter self-consciously draws attention to Standard English as a discourse, that is, as a political performance with a clearly articulated architecture of relations of domination and power that mediates the lives of those who speak it and who do not. Therefore, the fore-grounded aim of the letter is to be political more so than expressive. That is, it seeks to draw attention more to its form than it seeks to be open or communicative in a simple sense. True, it cannot help but signal its desire to communicate an interest, as would do the language of a letter by any speaker, be that person creole, local white, educated black, or anyone for that matter. As communication, however, its obvious aliveness to its medium should gesture rather violently to some desires, and probably genres being present other than letter writing, its obvious genus.

Two points immediately suggest themselves for consideration relating to the letter's position within the discourse of journalism, and its status as a peculiar kind of text juxtaposed to the surrounding text in the newspaper. First, the letter is in the realm of polemical literature, which challenges the status of the surrounding newspaper column as non-fictional (read realistic) and objective truth. Secondly, it brings its own standards and codes of interpretation that are grounded in the folk voice.

The 1877 letter, according to these ideas, points to the ideological content constituted in the use of Standard English in the text surrounding it. It also highlights the corresponding 'de/nigration' of creole (its designation as nigger talk). It does so by establishing that the universe of this linguistic discourse is irrevocably penetrated by diglossia, that is, it points to the fracture in the linguistic system where domination and oppression differentiate the social environment. In Bahktin's case the differentiation is by class, in ours differentiation is also by race and ethnicity.

The style of the letter recalls the tea meetings of old time Barbados spoken of in an earlier chapter, where speechifying using grand-sounding words is performed. In this performance, the vernacular voice makes obvious reference to its oppositional other—the 'standard' form and thus creates a double voice. Its double voice is also created in its implication of an expected vernacular-speaking audience that can respond as insiders, knowledgeable of the true nature of existing social relations of power, to the words being dropped. This tradition of double-voicing that the 1877 letter articulates fuels the irreverent laughter of the creole voice that Jeanette Layne-Clarke falls back on. Layne-Clarke presents as an icon of this voice the wide open mouth of Lick Mout Lou on the front cover of *Badinage*.

Jeanette Layne-Clarke:
who like to lick she mout*

Jeanette Layne-Clarke was a middle-class journalist who used Bajan creole to write for the news media, (print, radio and television) and whose work uses many of the strategies of the writer of the 1877 letter. Her written Bajan signals its differences from standard English by non-standard spelling of words; it uses the apostrophe to signal sounds of Standard English that are missing. In an interview she admitted that she deliberately used phonological spelling (2001).

Layne-Clarke graduated from one of the top prestigious secondary schools in Barbados: Queens College. She was also trained as a British Broadcasting Corporation (BBC) journalist. Layne-Clarke was therefore not ignorant of the strategies she was using, nor ignorant of the value placed on Barbadian Standard English (in fact on British Standard English as per the BBC), and correspondingly, on the oral voice and vocabulary of Bajan dialect. She knew that the latter is denigrated and the former highly praised and desired, yet being quite proud of her BBC English heritage, she was nevertheless a key figure that kept many older Bajan creole expressions alive through her writing.

I readily recognise that Layne-Clarke's work has the problematic tendency to present very few of the range of human emotions

---

* who like to lick she mout

  Who likes to talk/gossip

outside of anger and hostility. Consequently, her characters, predominantly women, tend to look rather stereotypical and narrow, although never stupid. She admittedly concentrated on the comical as her medium of communication and the satirical cackle as her signature voice (personal interview 2001). This sometimes takes the work into the realm of being brawling*, a characteristic that is problematically supposed by the elite of Barbadian society to be the low-rated and stereotypical behaviour of working class Barbadians. Therefore, as with the 1877 letter, there is a problematic relationship with the creole as used by Layne-Clarke, if one reads it in a particular way: literal and straight. But is this how the writer presents it to us? And is her intention the only thing we are expected to discover, if we can discover this? Is she not using a discursive practice that is far more sophisticated and imaginative? Should we not be looking to document a practice in all its variety and complexity, rather than pontificating about it using values that begin to sound rather patronizing and themselves classist and racist?

Layne-Clarke's characters are almost invariably working-class in origin, even when they inhabit roles like politician, secretary and the like which may normally attract classification as middleclass. Significantly, the abiding personality trait that Layne-Clarke upholds in her portrayal of these characters is their wicked insistence on their right to comment on every God thing in their universe! There is no coy or vapid "returning to

---

* brawling

 To be loud and abrasive

the true status of personality" by these characters. Lamming uses these quoted words to argue that the Caribbean peasantry achieved historicity through the West Indian novel, but he is rightly criticised for it by Gordon Rohlehr on the grounds that it portrays the West Indian folk as passive, inert and invisible until the appearance of West Indian novelists (Rohlehr *Strangled City* 54). Drawing on evidence by W. G. Sewell of peasants in the mid-nineteenth century, Rohlehr asserts that peasants can be shown to have been "struggling successfully to maintain the spirit of emancipation and to establish a certain independence from the plantation system" (54). Furthermore, as is argued here and as Rohlehr himself has extensively supported, popular forms like calypso and carnival have also encompassed this spirit of emancipation.

Creole narrative is the language of a people who are self-authorised and have been for generations. Layne-Clarke gives good example of just such self-authorisation in a piece where Punky Malone, the homosexual in *Pampalam*, insists on his right to comment on cricket even though he knows nothing about the game.

> "T'ree mo' wickets went quick-time,
> Wid Punky still runnin' 'e mout',
> Mistakin' Courtney Walsh fuh Benjamin,
> Counkin' Hick in when 'e was out...
>
> Dis time, Gladys, Dinks an' Vicey
> Was tryin' to follow de action,

> But de foolishness Punky was talkin'
> Was provin' to be a distraction.
>
> So suddenly, between de t'ree o' dem,
> Duh decide duh did had enough;
> Gladys tell Punky: "See You?
> Ef Yuh don' hush, I gine gi' you a cuff!"
>
> But Punky by now was enjoyin' 'eself
> In 'e new role as commentator,
> So 'e purse-up 'e lips to leggo some pips
> Sooner rather dan later.
>
> T'ree drag-swords like wunnah cyahn frighten me!
> Wunnah feel wunnah invent cricket?
> Ef my cricket terms en right, I don' give a shite...
> I pay fuh my blasted ticket!" (21)

Punky, like other users of creole narrative, is talking not only to 'air he mout' (that is, not just 'talking to hear he-self speak') although he is talking also for that purpose. His statement that he is authorised to talk because he "pay fuh he blasted ticket" suggests he would have been talking even if to experts and inventors of 'the white people game'. Punky is talking to let others hear him talking, to be **overheard**. He is talking to take up talking space. He is, in Lamming's words, taking an occasion for speaking, and not giving a shite* how others receive he as long as they know he talking, 'cause he is people too. As a consequence of this position, Punky exaggerates, he uses

---

* shite

A variation of 'shit', used especially in Ireland and the UK, and in Barbados

profane language, he chooses a role to execute a performance, and he expresses freedom. All of these ways of positioning himself are manoeuvres of creole narrative.

The possibility exists that Layne-Clarke may be manipulating creole to laugh at its speakers, but her laughter is certainly also at the expense of the official standard and its attempts to discipline speaking. After all, she got to speak publicly and to write in a way that, she always reminded her interviewers, she was constantly strictly forbidden to speak as a child. Therefore, Layne-Clarke has more going on than any attempt to parody creole. Her work can be equally read as an attempt to create space for herself as a woman writer in a competitive arena, by her choice of a genre—creole narrative—that predates her, and which takes its definition from its oppositional stance. It is an oppositional stance that lets her mock her own middle-class upbringing.

It could be suggested that Layne-Clarke is at the least laughing at homosexuals in her portrayal of Punkey, but again, even this can be viewed differently. Many homosexuals in Barbados effect public personas which they flaunt in the self-authorised manner of Punkey. Often critiqued as a self-righteous Anglican community, Barbados nevertheless is also known among many West Indians in the Caribbean as the homosexual capital of the Caribbean. A kind of albeit grudging acceptance of homosexuals obtained in Barbados, possibly because of the very public and oppositional stance many homosexuals have taken in the country as they have carved out a space for themselves. (Unfortunately this may be changing as a very violent homophobia fuelled by anti-homosexual dance hall reggae culture and a new Christian fundamentalism appears to be gaining ground.)

The Overheard

The occasion is serious compared to Punkey's predicament; however, the speech by the shoemaker in *Castle* as he takes opposition to one of Mr. Slime's investors who has come to dispossess him of his house, echoes Punkey's self-authorised grandstanding voice. The shoemaker too talks to be overheard. It lessens his sense of powerlessness to put up big talk even if he cannot turn back the circumstances. The new owner has just attempted to appease the Shoemaker by euphemistically naming what he is doing as "helping", and rather than continue the argument inside, the shoemaker has left his shop to stand and speak loudly and abusively outside on an embankment. In this spot the other villagers on the streets can not only see, but hear/overhear him:

> 'Help yuh mother's arse', the shoemaker said. 'Who want any f...g help from you?' ... 'You'll get into trouble,' the man said. 'I'll make things difficult for you if you haven't got respect.' 'Respect for who?' the shoemaker shouted. 'I've respect as when as I've got to have it, but for you, a two-colour shit-smelling bastard like you, what you talkin' 'bout respect. An' if you don't get off this blasted land before I count ten, if by the time I count ten you ain't off this spot o' land they'll hang me, the law'll hang me... You come on a big bright morning like this to tell me

some shitting story 'bout this spot belonging to you, an' I got to get off in how many days you says?' 'In three weeks,' the man said. 'Why God blind you; the landlord whatever he be never ever come telling anybody 'bout getting' off this land... You can call Jesus Christ 'imself to talk to me,' the shoemaker said. 'Send anybody you like to send, you mulatto shit-smelling son of a bastard' (234-235).

There is genuine anger but also a certain degree of grand-standing as the shoemaker uses several well-known Bajan profanities to curse off the invader. The statement 'big bright morning like this' is a Bajan stock phrase that is used in a comical way to emphasise the degree to which someone is being an irritant to the speaker. The Allsopp *Dictionary of Caribbean English Usage* identifies this use of the word 'big' as jocular. He gives the example: "'Dey should hide she away. Big Governor and t'ing coming and she comin' out in she nightgong'" (98). Therefore, the shoemaker's personal abuse of the invader shares somewhat the delivery and artistic purpose of Punkey's busing. Alongside whatever serious message the character might bring, the appeal to laughter is not far from the author's design. Lamming's humanizing of the shoemaker by dipicting him at the end of the scene with his tears falling onto a boot he begins to stitch is different from Layne-Clarke's strategy of showing only the one side of her characters. However, this difference does not invalidate the judgement that they both exploit a similar double voice that is rooted in folk laughter and the classic carnival pose of one thing forced to overhear another.

The selection of the name *Overheard* for the *Lizzie and Joe* series by Cordle signals this diglossic universe and is thus particularly fitting. In being given the language of Lizzie and Joe we are also given a frame for their discourse. That is the Standard English journalistic text surrounding it, and taking an active stance as a disciplinary agent against it. However, that standard is forced into the passive role as an over-hearer of another oppositional linguistic context.

Layne-Clarke's *Bajan Badinage* gives us another insight into this carnival rhetoric in her presentation of the politician as an archetype. Lamming also exploits this representation in *Castle*. In Layne-Clarke's poem "Call Me. Minister" (58-60), the minister of government character elaborates on how he now, with his ministerial status, is a person apart, "a veritable V.I.P", "one of a exclusive breed." The persona concludes:

> I got onderlings, minions, yardfowls
> Dat does treat me as if I's King Kong!
> To show duh respeck,
> dem does even genufleck-
> To dem I cyan do neffing wrong.
>
> So don' fail to address me as Mr. Minister-
> I en nuh Smitty nuh mo', get dah clear!
> But I know my cue, I's become one o' you
> Durin' a election year!"(60)

The minister is clearly not talking to any of the fictive onderlings*, minions or yardfowls*, despite his apparent address to them in the second stanza here. That would be political suicide. He is perhaps talking to a group of his drinking buddies or to his clique at a cricket match. In any event, he is overheard as well as heard. He is talking out from the stage to the audience at the performance, in a linguistic performance by Layne-Clarke that satirises politicians, in a voice that Barbadians would use to satirise politicians, but she gives that voice to the minister himself.

In this wicked portrayal, Layne-Clarke accomplishes two acts. She not only lays bare the real, recognisable and in Barbados often remarked on performance in which many politicians excel, that is of basking in the luminosity of political privilege. She also cynically refuses to allow the 'people' the easy demonising of politicians and the automatic 'angelicising' of themselves in contrast. She says in essence, "wunnah can't call back the Minister from his journey up the Nile of political privilege, because look how wunnah is participate in the dirty game of politics wunnaself!" In other words, she shows the onderlings* and yard fowls* (and perhaps the audience) to be equally good at this corruption that too often marks national politics in Barbados.

One hears echoes of this persona in *Castle.* This time the character is not a literal politician like Mr. Slime, but is his

---

* onderlings

    Barbadian creole word for 'underlings'

---

* yardfowls

    Barbadian creole word for a political sycophant

veritable mentor the landlord, equally a politician. With his masquerade display on the rooftop of his house and his Sunday afternoon carnival parades, the landlord tries to establish his distance to ensure that the minions, underlings and yardfowls that he thinks are the villagers of Creighton do not forget to address him as Mr. colonizer—a veritable V.I.P. and a breed apart. On the other hand, he finds it possible to become one of them when it is required, as in the case of his ideological repair work when he treats Ma as a confidant, "in intimate heart to heart talk" (Lamming, *Castle* 83) in order to disseminate the Caliban story, or with Ms. Foster when he serves her tea a la housetop style.

In the piece, "Corn Beef An' Biscuits Comin", Layne-Clarke emphasises the critique of the politician and the electorate. She castigates political candidates who seek to buy votes with handouts of corned beef and biscuits. This is a traditional appeal at election time in Barbados that some say plays on 'Barbadian' gluttony. In this poem, Layne-Clarke presents the now-wealthier (or more canny) low-income voter, demanding a more appropriate and expensive buy-out! The politician is to be castigated, but as this poem suggests, so too can be the voters.

> "But leh dem mek mocksport to get we support
> An' leh dem listen 'cause I talkin' plain-
> We en want nuh dam corn beef an' biscuits dis time
> Duh got to come wid caviar an' champagne!" (54)

The voters talking here conclude after analysis that the

politicians are playing them for fools, making 'mocksport'* at them. This awareness suggests that people do not passively let their votes be bought. They sell them, or at least, pretend to sell them. They also thereby buy jobs for themselves and their family members, paved roads in their districts, and scholarships for their children, all responses by parliamentarians using this mechanism of buying votes. In other words, people are really not just eating for a bellyful. They are making the most they can by adopting roles to their political advantage. In a corrupt bourgeois society where privilege is the currency for allocation of resources, this is a premeditated, doubling and clever strategy. It is also a strategy that abounds with irreverent laughter at the dominant system.

Linguistic Displacement

People are aware that it is very costly to have rebellions that overthrow systems. In the meanwhile, they use mechanisms to carve spaces where their needs are met. Even where their interest is not in rebelling at all, they do aim to widen their sphere of influence towards accessing more of the resources and goods which capitalism holds out before them as necessities of the good life.

The strategies outlined above remind us of the position taken by Mrs. Foster in *Castle* when she visits the landlord to get help

---

* mocksport

  teasing, heckling, making fun of someone by 'mocking' (imitating) them

when the flood destroys her house, and his response in offering her money and tea in a saucer and cup (Lamming, *Castle* 34). We can read her act of falling down on her knees to kiss the landlord's hand after he offers her a cup of tea and money as a sign of her self-hatred and internalised subordinate status. Lamming, like Layne-Clarke, could certainly be critiquing the folk for their collusion with a system that oppresses them. Alternatively, we can as easily read it as Mrs. Foster's act to sell her vote, figuratively speaking.

Like the minions, Mrs. Foster is showing the landlord respect by even genuflecting, he thinks, but she could be playing the yardfowl via linguistic displacement with the idea in mind that she needs her house fixed. Due to the rains at the beginning of the novel, Mrs. Foster has just lost her house and possibly her husband, and she is a woman with lots of children and no source of income that we know of. Her needs are great and the system of colonialism controls the resources she needs. If one recognizes that the landlord does not have to give her the response that he does and which she clearly finds appealing, then she may have turned him into a version of the politician having to appeal to and appease a vote-carrying constituent. The vote for which the landlord is asking is her continued vision of him as a saviour and master. He may have gotten it with the vivid symbol of her genuflection. However, this cannot be separated from Mrs. Foster's response when she next encounters the overseer, the landlord's agent and deputy. Immediately as Mrs. Foster leaves the landlord's presence she assails the overseer with an uncalled for (mental) 'busing'* (Lamming, *Castle* 34): "'When I come out and see the bad-minded black son-of-a-bitch we call the overseer, I shake my backside (God forgive me) at him, just to let 'im know that I was people too'" (34).

Is Mrs. Foster unaware that the overseer is a representative of the landlord's, his stand-in? Is her backside-shaking defiance only to tell the fellow black man that she is people too? Perhaps it is more. The latter becomes at this moment the face of colonialism which has been domesticated by creole narrative. This is the face in which it is more prudent to shake one's backside and assert one's 'people too' status if one is in as precarious a position as Mrs. Foster. Lamming validates this instance of linguistic resistance. Unless one can muster collective support for a more viable and dignified overthrow of systems of oppression it will have to do.

The scene with the boys talking about the penny and the empire is another incident of linguistic displacement and festive speech through what can be called the performance talk aspect of creole narrative. This aspect establishes that something else is being talked about in addition to or besides what appears on the surface of the talk. It is talk to deliver some other message. In this case the talk given to these boys by the writer domesticates the ideology of colonialism, if only in the boys' juvenile and incomplete way, and hence, distances it and makes it available

---

* busing

   the act of hurling abuse

for potential rejection.

The boys are given the pennies by the visiting colonial schools inspector as part of the celebrations of the queen's birthday (Lamming, *Castle* 42). They appear happy to receive them, but out of the earshot of the officials but well within their presence in the school classroom, they debate in fantastical hypotheses about how the king of England's face gets on a penny in Barbados. That they seek to know this at all, rather than just accepting it as natural, signals problems in the garden of colonial paradise. Secondly, it comes in the midst of Lamming's discussion on the stable ideological role of education in buttressing the colonial system and keeping Little England steadfast and constant to Big England (*Castle* 37); thus, it suggests that the debate is not quite innocent in the novel, nor is it meant simply to critique the uselessness of colonial education.

This serious play by these boys is a scene of their becoming. They begin a remaking of the other and hence of themselves. Here, they do not confirm what they have been taught or otherwise drilled in—that the king of England's head on Barbados's money, on even its most unpretentious coinage, is a natural, organic and right thing. The copper penny here represents these young boys, and the circumstances of their getting it point to the process that stamps them as the king's own. However, the boys seek the organic link of causality: maybe the king presses his face against each coin; maybe it was a photograph of the king's face stuck on every penny; maybe it was drawn on the copper by a pin when the copper was still soft from the melting process; maybe there was only one real penny ever made with the king's face and the others were imitations made by a kind of stamp (Lamming, *Castle* 53-55).

It is in this invention that the fact of the king's head on coins— colonialism's stamp on them who live so far from the king— is made un-natural, historical. In fact, several of the boys conclude at the end of the discussion that the king was never seen by anyone; the person seen was only a shadow king, like all Englishmen who were both men and shadow men. "But", they sum up, "you had to be careful when you had anything to do with English people. It was always difficult to distinguish between the man and the shadow, and sometimes it was all shadow" (Lamming, *Castle* 55).

The distancing involved in the conversation makes strange and hence domesticates a process that seeks ordinarily to make itself opaque and thus infuse them with otherness. Their lengthy debate about and unmaking of that process refuses otherness, and places them at the centre of meaning making. This conclusion is supported by the fact that the discussion moves from one on pennies to a discussion on the English colonizer. When one places the other references to money or pennies in the text next to this discussion, one senses that this discussion is about refusal of otherness and about creating meaning.

The scene of the boys' festival speech primes us to understand both the significance of the Penny Bank in the proposed future of the villagers and the final scene where money resurfaces. In the latter, rioters refuse to take the money in cash registers when they break into shops, despite the fact that the riots are very much about money, even if not exclusively so. We are told they leave bundles of it lying about on floors (Lamming, *Castle* 200). Given the sense of breakdown in law that is implied in the riots, this refusal is a curious and loaded act. It is less some altruistic or quixotic act than it is a trope for the rejection of the shadow king Englishman and his repressive signs.

The hypotheses the boys advance about the head on the penny seem particularly lacking in common sense even for five to six year olds, especially given the astuteness of their assessment of the true nature of social relations in the colonial situation. Lamming here either stereotypes the Black (children) as fools and lacking in basic knowledge and common sense, or he is using a technique of creole narrative, where the character talks mainly to expose the fact that talk and the capacity to define represent embattled ground. In other words, here the characters talk to be overheard. Even though the author does not use the boys' direct speech, we decipher from their indirect speech through the omniscient narrator's reportage that these characters are young warriors in that battle. It is as though they are overheard by the narrator. In addition, though the headmaster does not quite understand what they say, it is clear that he overhears them as he uses his whistle and its threat of colonial sanction to quiet the 'talk'. Would his whistle have been necessary if all were right in the colonial garden of 'Little Barbados?'

Two factors underline the irony of this money talk. When the headmaster gave the boys the coins, he said he hoped that they would do something "wise" with them, and to "think" before they spent the pennies, as the good Queen Victoria would have them do (Lamming, *Castle* 42). Secondly, the experiment the villagers devise to sever the material relations imposed by Queen Victoria and her lot involves something called a Penny Bank. Lamming therefore means for us to exploit the layers of meaning present in this irreverent laughter given to the boys, just as Layne-Clarke (and Punkey) means Punkey's talk about cricket to be ironic, even though he knows that he knows nothing about it and cannot be counted among its spokespersons in any meaningful way.

Lamming delivers his unmasking of education to expose it as domination, and makes his exposure of the relations of domination here mainly through the mechanism of creole festive speech. In the disobedient use of language on a topic they should have taken for granted, the boys distance the pennies as a sign. Consequently, they unmake the meaning of this sign, and remake that meaning according to a 'logic' which does not even bear resemblance to the concept 'logic.' While the chapter starts off as one that asserts the primacy and force of English education and English organization and control of the learning system, it ends with the boys' assertion that they use another kind of logic—their own—to receive this discursive pressure.

Festive Laughter in a Carnival Novel

We see a distancing/objectification and questioning similar to the boys' debate about the head on the penny, in Earl Lovelace's novel *The Dragon Can't Dance*. This is a novel about carnival in Trinidad, and Alderick, a main character, plays the mask of the dragon each year. Lovelace proposes that the costume making of carnival enables the character's enlivening. The act of building and rebuilding, the repeated restoration and destruction of the dragon's costume for the annual carnival, ultimately brings Alderick to consciousness about the true nature of his disabled life as a poor black living on Laventille Hill by enabling him to objectify that life.

Rather than simply playing the mask as a simple act of entertainment, Alderick comes to attention about the meaning of his actions in creating the dragon in relation to other things not happening in his life. He considers the 'fearsomeness' that he tries to play in his dragon mask and the power that the mask gives him, against various circumstances of lack in his life. He lacks a steady income and is unable to participate in the society in a way that validates his humanity. Posing this against the dragon mask that he plays every year, he begins to see that he needs to do more than 'act out' a 'power' that evades him in non-carnival time.

It may seem that Lovelace's story overturns the argument about the power that resides in the carnival. Here, it seems, is Alderick discovering that carnival is after all just making sport. This represents the character's perception of the carnival as catharsis according to the Aristotelian paradigm. It does not reflect the view of carnival as return of an order of equality and a promise of transformation. However, crucial contradictions exist between this view of Alderick's and the author's. The methodology and aesthetic choices Lovelace selects to resolve Alderick's dilemma are still very much in the vein of carnival as resistance and as an attempt to install a democratic regime, according to the utopian view.

For example, Alderick joins the men's lime at the corner of the street and engages the police in a face off as a way of asserting identity and resisting oppression. The limers at the street corner constitute a veritable carnival stick-fighting band. In the outcome of the love story between Alderick and the young girl from his neighbourhood, Lovelace also reaffirms Alderick's dragon performance at the carnival. She is not interested in him when he drops his dragon performance, but is moved to return to him once he understands that his playing the dragon is an important act of symbolic redemption for the community.

Carnival mask, Lovelace seems to be suggesting, allows the members of the labouring classes to carry on the real business of their social existence, to explore their social self and participate in power. In a history that sees working class gatherings as threatening to social order, the strategies that designate derision of hierarchal order/redistribution of resources/generating of income/entertainment are often co-joined and are worked out necessarily through mask.

In a way similar to the one Lovelace uses—through having the character halt and examine in detail a process that is ordinarily habitual and hence can be invisible—Lamming alerts us to how the villagers come to consciousness about the real social relations that construct them as colonized inferiors. The boys abandon the quest to discover exactly how the king's face gets on a penny, to become involved in another discussion that leads to important conclusions. They assert, "...newspapers usually printed what they thought people liked to hear" (Lamming, *Castle* 54); and finally, that the king and his family "were human like everybody else" (Lamming, *Castle* 55). These are important acknowledgements that will aid the struggle for freedom which the villagers desire. They point to the historicity of colonial society, to the fact that it was constructed and can be dismantled. They also point to the importance of storytelling in the creation of alternative histories, which is another strategy of creole narrative that Lamming uses.

Reliable Rumour

The second form of creole narrative that Lamming uses in *Castle* is what I call reliable rumour. This form is used to pass information important to people's understanding of their social environment and their authentic responses to it. It runs counter to official communication systems, including the education system and the press, which fail to deliver intelligence necessary for change. It is an alternative education process that has to happen if the long process towards self-emancipation begun during slavery is to advance with any success. Indeed, this alternative education process was produced by that very history as disenfranchised and oppressed social groups organised around their own survival. Through this unofficial and often, though not always, underground process, the oppressed staged their resistance against the humiliation that daily assaulted them under systems of colonialism and slavery, and continues to assault them under neo-colonialism.

Lamming gives an example of the existence of this unofficial process in an interview when he talks about the Moyne Commission hearings in Barbados that followed the 1930s disturbances (qtd. in Scott 78). The commission had set up microphones outside of Queen's Park house where the hearings were taking place to accommodate the crowds in attendance, and as a boy he had gone to the Park as part of that crowd. What Lamming recalls most about the occasion was how the crowds outside frequently interrupted testimonies by calling out, "That's not true! That's not true!" (qtd. in Scott 78). Even if their knowledge did not get into the official records, the crowds were ensuring that the Commissioners recognised that another history existed, and that they were overheard even if not officially heard.

In *Castle*, the real history about slavery comes to the boys through the same kind of unofficial talk. The school system does not teach about slavery; however, as they wait to be dismissed, one boy passes along the rumour that he has heard from an old woman that blacks were once owned by whites in the island (Lamming, *Castle* 70). In fact, the story seems to suggest that slavery continues: "The queen freed some of us but most of us are still slaves" (Lamming, *Castle* 70). Many of the children are sceptical about this, especially since the teacher whom they ask about it denies the rumour. The teacher says the old woman is wrong, and in any case, such things never happened in Barbados. This 'truth' is expected to stifle any urge for solidarity or any search for real self-knowledge and it appears to do so. The boys who "would choose the empire and the garden" go away satisfied in the explanation given (Lamming, *Castle* 72).

However, even if the young children do not quite believe the rumour, the adults who crowd along the school wall at the school's celebration also confirm the story about slavery having happened. This suggests that some informal system of education that keeps people knowledgeable about real social relations is going on. Lamming validates this informal system by having the village patriarch Pa dream the history of slavery (*Castle* 209).

The dream is presented as another story telling device that challenges colonial authorisation and authority. Pa's dream situates the riots in the context of the larger emancipation struggles. The dream is a recitation in creole, and like Kamau Brathwaite's long poem *The Arrivants*, records the history of the tribes before the slavers came, the middle passage which the enslaved endured, and the diasporic scattering. Thus, while the school system is invested in denying the history of colonial wrong and the emancipation struggle, the people maintain other mechanisms that keep them knowledgeable about important truths that colonial history occludes.

Similar intelligence about unrecorded histories that are important to the people is disseminated about the trade union activity which precedes and is important for the organization of the riots, the riots themselves, and the migration experience of the country. The latter is kept alive in the oral histories of the family migrations that G's mother shares with her son, and that Ma and Pa rehearse in conversation. Lamming is also engaging in this rhetorical strategy by his own instalments of unofficial history in this text which go a far way towards supplementing official histories of Barbados. In other words, he is utilizing creole narrative and intending to be overheard.

The point that Lamming wishes to establish is critical: there is internalisation by too many of the self-denigrating values imposed by colonial attitudes to black and poor peoples; nevertheless, the people themselves keep alive the means of their own self-empowerment. They do this by creation of alternative political/power structures and mediating institutions. The oral intelligence system of reliable rumour keeps the people aware and capable of working towards and generating change when they can afford it.

In a 1982 television interview with Vic Brewster of the Caribbean Broadcasting Corporation, Lamming remarks on the existence of these countervailing values and the vernacular systems that disseminate them (9 November 1982). He points to the economic independence of many of the people around the villages where he grew up. These people practised various crafts such as tailoring, shoe making, dressmaking, and various small-scale services and industries. His assessment was that people wanted to be self-employed and took great pride in being artisans. They did this work, he believed, expressly in order to avoid other jobs on the plantation or being messengers for town merchants. Artisanship offered them the possibility of earning some respect as opposed to the lot of being the butt of racist insults and those emanating from class that were endured by persons working for the elite white and coloured groups.

Lamming states in the interview, "I was very angry at the weight of deprivation placed on the poor" (qtd in Brewster 9 Nov. 1982). And the degree of these deprivations, coming after the experiences of slavery and balanced against the weight of expectations about emancipation, was hard to stomach. Social and economic conditions in the 1930s setting of the novel were nowhere near what people expected when they were told at emancipation that they could now be paid for labour expended. Work outside the plantation system was scarce and poorly paid, and encompassed conditions of labour that one scholar, George Belle, calls "paternalistic" and "almost pre-capitalist" (n.p).

Belle identifies that salaries of men working at the Barbados Foundary during the 1930's were 3c and under. Work on the plantation for those who stayed on tenantry land, like the villagers on the Creighton estate in *Castle*, was subject to continued high levels of exploitation, long periods of unemployment during the hiatus between crop seasons, and social and political abuse (Belle, n.p). Belle records that the local Dean Commission set up after the 1937 Revolt and before the Royal Moyne Commission, worked out a budget for an ordinary worker per week as follows:

Table 1

Budget for an Ordinary Worker	
Item	*Cost*
Food	$51.09c
Clothing	$44.64
Medicines	$8.30
Washing	$00.24
Fuel and Light	$17.05
House Rent	$00.39
Subvention to Friendly Soc.	$00.12

Source: Belle, "The Struggle for Political Democracy: 1937 Riots." 150th Anniversary Lecture Series III. Queens Park Bridgetown, Barbados. 17 Mar. 1987. n.p.

This gives a total of $126.83. In contrast to this, the weekly wage for the best paid plantation worker was $1.78c (Belle n.p.)

However, a countervailing critical factor for Lamming was the fact that these very people exercised their minds on their environments and were educated thereby. Through that process they created their own popular and other intellectuals who helped them to see ways to bring about change (qtd. in Brewster 9 Nov. 1982). Popular intellectuals, like the majority, experienced the weight of colonial race and class oppressions, but they named these experiences for what they were and for how they sought to deprive poor black people of their humanity. This ascription of meaning to the experiences they suffered was the centre and source of their alternative education processes. Lamming, an intellectual who self-consciously practices that art of ascribing meaning and independent definition to the experiences of the poor, describes for us the sources of such education. He said, "the environment educated me." (qtd. in Brewster 9 Nov. 1982).

4   Calypso Aesthetic in Castle: Lamming the Kaisonian

Fig. 1. The Mighty Gabby singing calypso
Source: www.courses.vcu.edu/Images/calypgabby.html

When Lamming structures *Castle* the way he does by focusing on the poor and working class in the society he constructs and taking on board their concerns, language and discourses, he is easily identified as a 'political' novelist. This conclusion is essentially based on an exploration of his theme of anti-colonial struggles. What is not as easily recognized is the extent to which he delves into folk forms to provide both architecture and language by which to give form to his critical social theory and to express his aesthetic.

The tools at Lamming's disposal in the 1930s-1950s expressed his creole heritage, though they were also informed by the Caribbean history of colonialism. On the one side is the inherited English/Victorian novel form with two signal features: its "premeditated" structure, according to Kamau Brathwaite, and its concern with exploration of the individual ego and its struggle for fulfilment in the context of an existentialist alienation (*Jazz* 107). On another side, Lamming has for his use a creolised African tradition that is centred in the rhythms, values and concerns of the folk, and which is forged from a history of prohibition, resistance and celebration against all odds. The working class at the bottom and centre of West Indian society expresses these experiences in several ways, utilizing the media of performance to do so. In these practices of social performance—music, drama, dance and combinations of these—meanings, identities and boundaries are negotiated and transformed. These performances then provide rich resources from which West Indian writers draw to explore the culture and experiences of a people. *Castle* is an archive and repertory of some of these performances. One that engages attention is the calypso.

George Lamming's *Castle* creatively mediates the text of prose fiction with a transgressive aim in mind—the English form is made to submit to/integrate with the folk form, much as the calypso spins its own take on the community's history. *Castle* invades the individual act of reading with elements of calypso; it thereby encourages a kind of recognition. The fact that Caribbean critics have not seen this is the degree to which working class cultural forms like calypso remain in large measure outside academia. It seems reasonable to think that such inclusion could meaningfully contribute to the regular teaching programmes of the university. It could contribute to widening the domain of mediation that is critical practice.

If the working class nature of West Indian literature is indeed fore-grounded, then we can see continuities between it and other forms of working class theorizing such as happens with calypso, as we have shown here.

This chapter examines the influence of calypso as a special form of creole narrative in the novel *In the Castle of My Skin*. The argument is not that Lamming self-consciously drew on this popular form, but that he is influenced by it. As stated in the introduction, what the writer effects and what he intended do not have to equate. In the case of this novel, the debt to calypso is there despite the fact that Lamming in the interview with this writer stated that the song in Barbados was the Anglican hymn rather than the calypso. While this may be true, the following critique is based on the idea that Barbadians sometimes used the Anglican hymn in ways very similar to the picong calypso form. The creative solutions Lamming and popular artistes like the calypsonian the Mighty Gabby offer evolve out of the same social and political conditions, and arise from the same need in an era of late colonialism to discover what it would mean to exercise freedom in a society and culture of one's making. When one examines the structures, themes and motifs of the popular form, the similarities appear too many and too profound to be merely coincidental.

Critics have failed to explore these connections in Lamming, as they have too completely labelled him a political novelist with a Marxist bent. Such a label has precluded meaningful discussion of, for example, humour in Lamming's novels. Yet *Castle* cannot be read without recognition of the significant aspects of humour, a major strategy of calypso, in this work. In this sense, this study opens up a debate that others may find fruitful to engage.

It should be admitted that the investigation in general terms is not entirely new. It contributes to the strategy of theorising Caribbean literature through cultural perspectives borrowed from popular music culture. Kamau Brathwaite makes one of the best-known efforts in this area in his identification of linkages between the popular African-American musical form, jazz, and Caribbean literary aesthetics (*Roots*). Brathwaite closely examines selections of West Indian literature in counterpoint to jazz, and plots major overlaps between the two forms (*Roots* 55-58). He identifies similar themes of protest and comfort, and affirmation at the brink of chaos in the two (Roots 55-58). He also shows how structural elements of community rhythms, improvisation, and call and response similarly occur in jazz and in the forms and concerns of certain West Indian texts.

Brathwaite argues that the West Indian writer (of the 1950-1960s) was beginning to express the same ethos and practices based on the New World experience: "that joy, that protest, that paradox of community and aloneness, that controlled mixture of chaos and order, hope and disillusionment [which are] at the heart of jazz" (*Roots* 63). He justifies his comparison with jazz on his belief (at the time) that no Caribbean music the equivalent of jazz existed. He believed that calypso, one popular form that he could consider, was only incidentally concerned with protest, having "no suggestion of alienation, no note of chaos", being "basically a music for dancing" (*Roots* 59). While I support Brathwaite's argument that African-American Jazz holds much in common with many Caribbean literary texts, like critic Curwen Best, I contest his conclusion that calypso is not a music of alienation and resistance, and therefore not capable of interpreting the literature of a region for which these concerns have been of paramount interest (Best, *Popular Music* 15).

Keith Warner takes up Brathwaite's lead in a chapter entitled, "Calypso in Literature", in his book, *Trinidadian Calypso: A Study of the Calypso As Oral Literature* (123-138). He provides important insights about how Samuel Selvon in several of his works and V. S. Naipaul in *Miguel Street* have drawn on the world of calypso to create characters and to denote a certain type of speech. Warner rightly identifies that these writers create a context for meaning in these calypso creations, as they draw on shared non-verbalized assumptions existing in the world of the calypso competition (126). However, as the title of Warner's book suggests, his main concern is with analyzing the calypso as oral literature and not with focusing on the written literature and showing linkages there.

Kwame Dawes is another critic who makes the music literature connection. In a 1999 text entitled *Towards a New Reggae Aesthetic in Caribbean Writing*, he analyses examples of West Indian literature for their music connections. However, the connection he explores is with Jamaican reggae music. Therefore, the analysis of how calypso influences West Indian literature continues to represent an undeveloped area of scholarship. This study hopes to address that shortcoming.

The analysis that I propose has significant advantages. First, it reconnects the spheres of popular culture (in this instance calypso) and high culture (literature). Caribbean civilisation is hardly served by these imposed class distinctions. Secondly, it lends ways of reading the literature by familiar structures of meaning in the calypso, and is thereby able to respond to a legitimate challenge issued by Lamming in the chapter "Western Education and the Caribbean Intellectual" of the book *Coming Coming Home: Conversations II*. Lamming challenges those who critique the Caribbean book, and hence potential occupants of what he calls a "domain of mediation" to extend the terrain of mediation, and in so doing also make the Caribbean text the possession of the total society (*Coming Home* 17).

Lamming's challenge hinges on his inclusive definition of who constitutes "the intellectual" in Caribbean society. He widens the traditional definition to include a previously excluded category, the Caribbean working class (*Coming Home* 19). He argues that the intellectual can also be the fisherman, the farmer, and I add, the calypsonian: all those in fact who, in the ordinary and extraordinary exercise of their daily work, develop discriminating judgments that have the capacity to extend beyond their immediate contexts to the wider society (with sometimes transformative consequences). For examples of the kinds of contributions that these other intellectuals can make, Lamming draws on work by Professor Woodville Marshall. Marshall argues that it was the Caribbean peasants who brought the feudalistic colonial plantation economies into the modern era by their alternative subsistence strategies and their establishment of villages, markets, churches and schools at the end of slavery (qtd. in *Coming Home* 19).

For Lamming, the terrain of mediation is the area where vital links can be forged, as he says, "between sources of knowledge and the wider consumption of facts" (*Coming Home* 18). It is a critical domain that supports the development of social and cultural sovereignty and the struggle to redeem the personhood/humanity of those politically, economically and culturally harmed by oppressive colonial history (*Coming Home* 17). In the domain of mediation, knowledge brokers can use the tension generated between experience and the imperatives of the dominant ideology to breach the boundaries of their discipline and hence extend the terrain of mediation.

Therefore, in *Castle*, for example, Lamming juxtaposes plantation landlords' demands and villagers' experiences of lack and diminished control vis-à-vis the plantation, to show how this feeds their land hunger and causes them to look to the education system for solution. Peasants invest in a system over which they do not initially have full control in order to make themselves economically mobile. They recognise that they must first mediate power, influence and resources in order to invest in land. Slime is one fulfilment of this strategy. G the scholarship winner but emerging committed intellectual is another. Lamming also demonstrates that those "down below" also debate this strategy when he inserts the striking workers from the city into the village in a potential conflict, and in his resolution of the Slime character as a betrayer. He demonstrates the debate also in his depiction of the Thumper character as one who enlarges the class nature of the debate to include its wider race configurations.

It is not simply a false consciousness that turns the villagers to the alienating system of education for a solution. Indeed, education is organized to reproduce the status quo, and hence is only concerned with disseminating information for the consumption of the individual with no attention to collective emancipation of the peasants. However, it is a potential domain of mediation and Lamming endows the peasant characters with this knowledge. Despite his eventual failures, it is an ex-teacher, Mr. Slime, who is able to draw on the folkways to establish the Penny Bank and Friendly Society, two institutions that show great possibility for satisfying the villagers' dreams. It is the folk themselves who have created the models that could potentially generate enough funds to invest in wide-scale land purchase, but they depend on the knowledge base of the school system to further that dream. Mr. Slime, who successfully masters that system, uses their vision of the transforming possibilities of education to successfully extend the domain of mediation even though, as we shall see, he appropriates the benefits for himself. What is important is the intellectual breadth of the vision of the peasants.

My intervention in bringing the calypso and *Castle* together participates in another attempt to widen the domain of mediation. Lamming rightly recognises that when Caribbean critics started to examine Caribbean literary texts they captured what he called "an acre of ground" for the text of the region, by designating it a phenomenon worthy of serious investigation in the classical curriculum (Lamming, *Coming Home* 18). In other words, one possibility for extending the terrain of mediation was revealed. Our history and society were founded on the repression of the indigenous and subsequently the creole culture and language of a majority of the population. This culture and language were long denied access to 'authorized' media. Hence, the appropriation by Caribbean writers of the textual space in the name and language of that majority was indeed a radical act. The penetration by these texts into the curriculum and the academic critical context represented a further victory. However, as Lamming bemoaned in the chapter on the Caribbean intellectual (*Coming Home* 18), and as Trinidadian novelist Earl Lovelace was to repeat at a Conference of West Indian Literature Teachers in 2001, this engagement has had little if any continuity beyond the enclave of the classroom. The coming to sovereignty of the literature, whereby the text becomes the possession of the total society, helped here by the critic, remains a project of the future (Lamming, *Coming Home* 18). This study hopes to intervene here also.

Lamming's inclusive definition of the intellectual implies that whether he consciously set out to do this or not, he was influenced by popular reflection and theorising by the very models on which he drew to create *Castle*. He does not take his models for prose fiction only from the English text, but also draws heavily upon popular forms including the calypso. He makes arguments elsewhere that suggest he is certainly aware of the calypso literature association. In an article published in 1966 entitled: "Caribbean Literature and the Black Rock of Africa", Lamming draws clear parallels between the West Indian novel and calypso. He specifically argues that like the calypsonian, West Indian novelists are close to the whole body politic; they are close to important occasions of the community, and this engenders "reciprocity of action between the writer and his (sic) immediate neighbourhood" (47). He sees this as the essence of calypso, and argues that the calypsonian is the "musical counterpart of the novelist" (46). It is not unreasonable, therefore, to look for a calypso framework to impact on the form and content, the syntax and the lexicon of the novel that Lamming brings. He obviously has thought about these connections, and in his search for a new form of the novel in which to explore his own concerns and the concerns of his society, it is not difficult to imagine that he would marry the two.

Nevertheless, it must be stated that Lamming denies that such an influence consciously existed for him at the time of writing *Castle*. In one of the interviews with this writer, Lamming cautioned that the calypso was not a presence in Barbadian culture at the time of the writing. He argued that the Anglican hymn was the common song, the "work-song" according to him, of the all sectors of Barbadian population (10-August-2005).

It can be agreed that the Anglican hymn was a central feature of Barbadian song culture; however, two counters can be made to the suggestion that it excluded the calypso ethic from the country. The folk song also played a significant part in the music culture of the society, and these were very similar to calypso in many of their expressions and functions as supported in the chapter of this study entitled "Gender Relations in *Castle*". Furthermore, Barbadians also used hymns in a subversive way. Hymns were not only sung in praise and worship or to uplift the soul as an aspect of spiritual expression. Hymns were also used to make arguments, settle arguments or drop message to an antagonist in a quarrel in the picong* fashion of calypso. In a personal interview, Barbadian actor and radio talk show host Tony Thompson corroborated this practice (27-10-2005). He placed my request for information on this practice on air and several other persons also confirmed it.

Thompson gives a brilliant example of the unorthodox use of Anglican hymns to quarrel by his two aunts, one married and the other not. The married aunt, to clinch an argument by pointing to the stigmatised status of spinsterhood that her sister bore, would sing all the Anglican wedding hymns she could recall. This would silence the spinster aunt for some time until she found her own hymn. The spinster would open her window wide and regale the household and community with the singing of the hymn, "Abide With Me". Knowing it to be a popular funeral hymn, she used this song to reinforce the (unspoken) message that, married or unmarried, all have to die (Thompson 27-10-2005).

If Barbadians did not have calypso, they certainly used the

---

* picong

    a form of verbal warfare used in calypso that shares an African history with games of insult such as the African-American tradition of 'the dozens'

hymn in unorthodox ways that significantly resembled some of the uses of the calypso. Even in *Castle* we see Lamming using this strategy. We recall that when the boys are trying to hide from the overseer who chases them after they are discovered on the grounds of the plantation, they attempt to hide in the street church meeting. In setting the scene for the call to salvation by the participants of the religious meeting, the narrator tells us "the women knew what hymn suited the particular incident" (Lamming, *Castle* 179). The final hymn, though solemnly introduced, echoes with the words of the narrator that the women know the right hymn for the occasion. "Into my heart,/ Into my heart,/Come into my heart, Lord Jesus" may mean what the church meeting's surface text says about the solemn occasion of repentance and salvation and the boys taking Jesus into their hearts; however, it may also mean that all acquiesce in letting the boys into their hearts/midst to conceal them. They enter the masquerade the boys are definitely engaged in, in order to hide them.

Another justification for the approach used in this chapter of linking calypso to text has to do with the fact that calypso itself is a creole Caribbean form like the culture which the novel seeks to explore. Calypso draws its structure from the African and French cultures of the past; it draws its music from French, English, Irish, African and creole Caribbean forms; and it borrows and builds on musical instruments from Europe, Africa and the creole Caribbean. It is not difficult to imagine that the West Indian novel could have a matching genealogy.

This strategy of relating calypso to West Indian literature is itself expressive of the very essence of hybridity, and therefore should be a particularly fruitful strategy to adopt.

Criticism such as will be attempted here is a way to demystify and draw the critical act and the text it explores into familiar ground for popular understanding and engagement. Lamming was working with the novel as a form which was/is very separate from the populace whose interests he defends. Therefore, it becomes necessary, if the book is to fulfil the intervention objective which Lamming clearly has, that popular possession of the text must be possible. The analysis of its folk form structures facilitates this as such critique both validates the work's objectives and merges form with function. In other words, if the people's lives are to be addressed, then their forms of articulating, not just their dialect but also their discourses, like calypso, could not have been avoided in the production of the text. Equally these forms cannot be avoided in the critical act as it helps to give the text into their possession.

This critical practice articulates one of the oldest traditions of Caribbean struggle, ambush under the performance of a vernacular strategy in order, hopefully, to widen the domain of critical mediation. Historians and other cultural theorists of the region have long established that popular song and accompanying dance activities have been utilised by African-descended Caribbean people to rehearse and plot insurrections against slavery and colonialism. As Gordon Rohlehr notes, citing D. Epstein, J. Handler and C. Frisbie, major rebellions under slavery were planned taking advantage of these song and dance activities (*Calypso and Society* 3). Two of the largest of these—the 1739 South Carolina rebellion and the Easter Sunday 1816 uprising in Barbados—are believed to have been plotted at dance assemblies. Ambush in this instance is the critique of a canonical text using a creolised form of criticism.

Calypso Form and Function

Most researchers of the calypso tell us that it takes its form from the West African "canoe-song" of social commentary, which the enslaved Africans had transported to the Caribbean in their forced migration to this region (Rohlehr, *Calypso and Society* 2). Referring to research by Dena Epstein, Rohlehr describes the characteristics of the typical traditional canoe-song as a litany or call and response form, constructed in couplets with a chorus, which is sung to drum accompaniment. This song stresses the elements of creativity and extemporaneity, and focuses on themes of love intrigues, praise of some beauty, or satirical social commentary (Rohlehr, *Calypso and Society* 2).

Apart from a few changes, calypso has retained many of the features identified. The couplet and chorus of the canoe-song has changed to a narrative verse of several lines and a repeated chorus. Many other musical instruments have been added, including the steel pan created in Trinidad. Another shift is that extemporaneity is no longer a central feature. In recent years it has been restricted to a sub-form, as not all calypsonians use it, and generally the few who do, append it to the end of a song during competition. The calypso continues to be judged by the elements of colour, wit and humour, which are rendered through the skilful use of simile, metaphor, irony, and double entendre. The deployment of the latter is to camouflage (or at least pretend to camouflage) outrageous remarks (Hill 68).

Arising out of an oral tradition, calypso blends entertainment with social commentary. Singers use it to 'send message' or 'drop talk' in the vernacular. In this way they can accomplish several goals: satirize social rules or the behaviour of authority figures; engage in spreading scandal; criticize the state and its failures; or conversely, they can offer praise and support for some political party, ideology or even themselves. All in all, the calypso can express a people's philosophical consciousness or their conceptions of the meanings and principles of their existence.

The following calypsos share several features with Lamming's *Castle*, including the designation of being political forms: *The Strike* by Atilla the Hun (qtd in Rohlehr, *Calypso and Society* 203); *Advice to West Indians* by Growling Tiger (qtd. in Rohlehr, *Calypso and Society* 212); and *Sedition Law or Warning to the Rich and Poor* by King Radio (qtd in Rohlehr, *Calypso and Society* 202). These calypsos were written during the period of the late 1930s, and all comment on the labour uprisings that raged over the Caribbean in the period 1935 to 1938. These calypsos address the same issue of the strikes which is a major theme that Lamming addresses in *Castle* (except for Sedition which, though it is written in 1938, sings about the Sedition Law of 1920).

Denunciations of *Castle* followed its initial production much as calypso has traditionally suffered. Hence, these calypsos are also selected to show how defiant the form could be even in a period of the most stringent attempts to ban and otherwise control it. Those attempts at control took several forms: police surveillance of calypso tents in 1930; enforcement of an old nineteenth century ordinance that tents end performances by 10:00 pm; the offering of a $15 reward (a significant sum at the time) by a newspaper, the *Daily Mirror,* "to anyone giving information to this newspaper which leads to conviction in a court of law of any 'chantrel' who sings nasty songs about a private citizen" (Rohlehr, *Calypso and Society* 278-279). Other measures of control, Rohlehr identifies, are the passage of the Theatre and Dance Halls Ordinance 1934-1935, which specifically targeted calypso in two of its items; and the request in 1938 of the Carnival Improvement Committee that all calypsos be submitted for censorship before they were performed (*Calypso and Society* 279).

Rohlehr notes that during this time many calypsos were restricted to avoid outright confrontation in face of the real danger of seizure and incarceration of composers (*Calypso and Society* 202). However, several calypsonians still made unmistakable statements of protest. The song called *Sedition Law or Warning to the Rich and Poor* by King Radio advises:

> "If a man want to be versed in politics
> He have to be plucky with a lot of tricks
> He has got to use a little diplomacy
> Mix up with commonsense and psychology"
> (Rohlehr 202).

We can see the characterisation of the local politician as an Anancy character being very clearly drawn. It is the mould from which a character like Mr. Slime can be said to be drawn. On the other hand, Radio's chorus more directly names the nature of the problem. He identifies the oppressive nature of the Sedition Law by stating that the authorities want "to license me mouth, dem na want me talk" and "license me foot dem na want me walk" (Rohlehr *Calypso and Society* 202). Atilla the Hun in his song, *The Strike*, disagrees with violent confrontation, calling the 1930s strikes and riots "a regrettable affair", but his sympathy towards the striking workers cannot be suppressed. Although he says, "...I don't know who is right or wrong", he declares:

> "All I know is that the wages too low
> And tribulation the workers have to undergo
> And we know – we all know the times are bad
> We want better conditions in Trinidad"
> (Rohlehr, *Calypso and Society* 203)

The Growling Tiger in his song *Advice to West Indians* tells West Indians to join together with other workers to fight for their cause. He advises that this is the "only" means to achieve their rights and protect themselves from domination and exploitation. Lamming's city rioters make similar observation. Tiger says:

> "I am advising every worker as a West Indian
> To be careful and join a labour union
> It's the only way you can achieve your right
> And to stop the oppressive hands of might
> And allow your progressive march to be an inspiration
> To the rising generation"
> (Rohlehr, *Calypso and Society* 212).

Not all calypsos are as concerned to make such political commentary. As noted, scandal and ribaldry are also very much part of the character of the form. Besides individual calypsos, a whole genre, the calypso drama, was developed in the 1930s in the service of such themes (Rohlehr, *Calypso and Society* 134-138). These dramas highlighted for ironic mockery the failures, weaknesses, private affairs and questionable pride of the social elite. For example, in 1933 a famous drama was the Divorce Drama on the issue of the first divorce case in Trinidad and Tobago (Rohlehr, *Calypso and Society* 137). Rohlehr records that in the 1930s divorce was to provide "enormous fodder for the calypsonians' talent at mocking the great." (*Calypso and Society* 137) An example is a calypso composed by King Radio in 1933, on the police commissioner, A. S. Mavrogordato's adulterous liaison with a married upper-class white woman (qtd in Reiss, *Music* 22). This may well have done much to spark police censorship of the content of calypsos. In fact, such performances so unsettled the elite that they attracted the attention of the legislators, who included calypso dramas among the list of "censorable performances" in The Theatre and Dance Halls Ordinance of 1934 (Rohlehr, *Calypso and Society* 137). In this regard, the story about the head teacher's adulterous wife in *Castle* reflects commentary and aesthetic choices calypsonians have historically used and fall within codes which audiences of the calypso have long been primed to recognise.

Calypso and *Castle*

From as early as the title of the novel, we see Lamming giving notice of his intention to 'send message' in the best calypso tradition. Here he signals several of the themes with which he will be concerned. *In the Castle of My Skin* draws notice to the English proverb which says 'a man's home is his castle', and signals Lamming's use of the calypso's trope of double entendre to point to several concerns. Even as he highlights the colonial subject's dispossession of material home/land, and that subject's entombment in an internalised racist definition of the self, he asserts the internal re-valorisation that is needed for the self's survival and development. The Longman Drumbeat publication of *Castle* carries the following quote on the back cover that supports this reading:

> "No black boy wanted to be white, but no black boy liked the idea of being black. When you asked Boy Blue why he was so black he would answer 'just as I was goin' to born the light went out.' The light had gone out for many of us" (Back cover).

There is a self-knowledge that these villagers must come to, including acceptance of the reality of their history and the fact of their connection to Africa. That self-acceptance must also be accompanied by a true reckoning of how and why the light had gone out, who had put it out, and the extent of their culpability in the continuing darkness. Villagers find that in addressing these issues, material possession, owning one's castle, is not an unproblematic goal. There is no doubt that Lamming supports the need to redress the land hunger of the poor, a condition rooted in imperialism/control by the English crown in its castle. However, he is not optimistic about the way the new native elite are moving to attend to the issue. Therefore he interrogates bourgeois materialism in the way he treats the middle-class and its values in the novel by using the calypsonian's techniques for scandalizing the 'great' to achieve his point.

Scandalizing the Great

In *Castle* the Landlord/colonialist and the other whites stand at the apex of those constituting the 'great'. Included in this classification is the gatekeeper class which arises from among the people, particularly through education or special favour granted from above. Social gatekeepers, the latter perceive themselves as having attained preferred status, as they had imbibed the culture of what the narrator calls the "world of the others' imagined perfection", and see their fellow villagers not privy to this status as the "enemy" (Lamming, *Castle* 26-27). The gate-keeper class includes the village overseers, civil servants, doctors and lawyers, headmaster and teachers. Lamming targets these characters and lampoons them in much the same way that the calypso and calypso drama exposed their prototypes to ridicule.

An early and telling example of Lamming's ridicule of the 'great' is a sharp vignette between the supervisor of the public baths and the schoolboys who are taking a collective bath. The supervisor's sombre officiousness is placed in absurd contrast with the mischievous competition between the quietly laughing boys as to who could hold his penis up "like a main spring"! (Lamming, *Castle* 29) In his meticulous attention to all that is happening in his domain, the supervisor catches the boys and righteously banishes them. He then goes back to his table where "he wr[ites] in his notebook hurriedly, indignantly... His head like the scrawling pen seem[s] to totter" (*Castle* 30). While he creates this record that he finds important enough to document, the supervisor is captured by the narrator in an emotional interior monologue in a state of deep anxiety quite out of proportion to the triviality of the incident. He agonises over how these people are there only "to get me into trouble. That's what they're like. You can never take chances, never, never, never" (*Castle* 30). The whole tone of this incident emphasises for us that we are to read this character as foolish and pompous.

The headteacher and the education system he oversees provide other sources of mockery. The scene is mentioned earlier in relation to another point where the headteacher proudly officiates over the visit by the white English schools' inspector. The attending pomp and ceremony of the occasion signals its importance. However, on this occasion, what is displayed as the epitome of the boys' learning is their ability to faultlessly recite in a rhyming song the spelling of the words 'crab' and 'go', and to repeat a local ditty on the number of days in the months. This, the narrator tells us, is information that the boys had been learning for the past three months.

A good example of a similar calypso critique of the colonial education system is The Mighty Sparrow's *Dan is the Man*. In this calypso, Sparrow satirizes the kind of repetitive children's stories from England which were used to teach West Indian children how to read. The stories and rhymes are contained in the choruses:

> "According to the education you get when you small
> You'll grow up with true ambition and respect from one and
> all
> But in my days in school they teach me like a fool
> The things they teach me I should be a block-headed mule
>
> (Chorus):
> Pussy has finished his work long ago
> And now he resting and thing
> Solomon Agundy was born on a Monday
> The Ass in the Lion skin
> Winkin Blinkin and Nod
> Sail off in a wooden shoe
> How the Agouti lose he tail and Alligator trying to get
> Monkey liver soup

The poems and the lessons they write and send from
England
Impress me they were trying to cultivate comedians
Comic books made more sense
You know it was fictitious without pretence
But like Cutteridge wanted to keep us in ignorance

(Chorus):
Humpty Dumpty sat on a wall
Humpty Dumpty did fall
Goosey Goosey Gander
Where shall I wander
Ding dong dell... Pussy in the well
RIKKI... TIKKI TAVI
Rikki Tikki tavi"
(qtd. in Brown, Morris and Rohlehr, 129-130).

The inclusion in the choruses, along with English stories and rhymes, of Afro-creole Anancy tales about the agouti and the alligator and the monkey, show how misbegotten is the imposition of the English education system and how irrepressible the culture it is seeking to dominate. The imposition of the English culture on the Afro-creole context and worse, in ignorance of that culture's stories and values does not just create a muddle, but inflicts vital errors, omissions and gives space for laughter to emerge in both Sparrow's song and Lamming's story about education. When what the boys learn for three months is put in the context of information given by the narrator that they had been taught in the school that slavery never occurred in Barbados, not only is Lamming scandalizing the education system for its gross misdirection, he is ridiculing the head and teachers as privileged functionaries in that system. They could after all have impressed the inspector even more if they had chosen to really teach something of more consequence.

Further, to stress how ridiculous are 'the great' in the scene described above, the author allows us to learn from a boy whom the headteacher has just brutally whipped at the end of the student's display that the head's wife beats him. In the paternalistic world being drawn, such a turnaround in gender violence is clearly ridiculous rather than tragic, and so Lamming presents it. The irony is underscored by the fact that the boy was being whipped for laughter about Queen Victoria's underwear. The head keenly protects the Queen's honour, but can offer his 'honour' no protection due to the intimacy of village life.

The boy has been privy to the story because his mother is the head's household worker. The story goes that after one beating the head rushes out on his verandah shouting to his neighbour in vernacular, "Woolah, woolah she put them pon me!" (52) The neighbour to whom he tells this asks him where he left his grammar, and the narrator says "…but he couldn't hear nothing but his own voice saying, 'woolah, woolah, she put them pon me!'" (52) Given his status as a member of the educated elite, a character like a headmaster is hardly likely, even in the context of realistic fiction, to use the creole dialect in this way, as it is scorned as 'broken' language. Therefore its use by the head in these circumstances, not to mention the neighbour's wry response, is obviously chosen for its comic effect by Lamming, a comic effect that squarely directs our laughter at this 'great'. It may even be that this is just another story doctored by the villagers for their own resistive amusement.

When the teacher at the school assembly drops the envelope, the head is driven into a paroxysm of fear and embarrassment that impels him into a long reverie, and heightens the sense of how ridiculous he appears. He nervously meditates on his life and the villagers' attitude toward him; on the inspector's possible reaction if he were to seek to discipline the teacher; on his future image in the light of whatever decision he makes. Lamming takes seven and a half pages to record these thoughts in internal monologue and still the head makes no decision on the pictures. In a further six pages, interspersed with normal goings on in the school, the scene shows the head finally left alone with the teacher he suspects, and still nothing happens.

Here, the narrator apparently abandons the matter. We recall, though, that such affairs had furnished prime material for calypsos and calypso dramas in those early 1930s that Lamming is portraying. Calypsonians sang of them to ridicule the island elites, scorn their moral and social hypocrisy, and undermine their political authority. This calypso inter-text saves the narrator from having to belabour the incident, and it makes the political weight of the story fully apparent to the initiated reader. It further frees the narrator to show some sympathy toward the head teacher in his personal disquiet. The human sympathy does not disturb the incident's wider social and political implications identified above, because these are already fully established by the critique elaborated in this particular calypso tradition.

The Love-intrigue Tale: Allegory of Freedom

Cuban writer and critic Antonio Benitez-Rojo correctly argues that the theme of Caribbean myths is "an archetype of 'liberation' that places us in conflict with any form of oppression." (452) I add to this, any form of orthodoxy. But this attitude is not simple. On the one hand, Caribbean people can be said to have absorbed and idealized certain values and ideologies of the plantation system and colonial society: for instance, the way we view marriage that is condoned by the state as an ideal. On the other hand, we jump at the opportunity to support values that oppose these ideals. An example is the high incidence of female-headed households across the region which bespeaks a preponderance of non-marital conjugal arrangements. This kind of contradiction often leaves Caribbean subjects with a kind of social schizophrenia as the only option for survival. Such conflict is clearly borne out in the confrontation between men and women, which calypsonians have traditionally seen as a fruitful area for commentary that *Castle* too exploits.

Calypsonians have established over the years stock images of women and men. There is the sweet-man/macho man, who has many women and is wedded only to the notion of perpetual bachelordom (Rholehr, *Calypso and Society* 222). Conversely, there is an attempt to disseminate an image of women as unfaithful, money-hungry, and generally evil—all women that is, except mothers (those at least whose children all have one father).

Rohlehr places this conflict between men and women in calypso in the 1930s and 40s in an economic context (*Calypso and Society* 216-218). Whereas western bourgeois expectations determined that a man should provide for a woman and children in a marriage, and that a woman should be a housewife and homemaker, in fact, both men and women faced realities of unemployment, poverty and hunger which made these ideals unworkable. Calypsonians expressed the anxiety which men in this context faced in calypsos such as Zeigfield's *Depression* sung in 1938.

> "Five children and a wife and myself to mind
> But to me the world is so unkind
> No work no food no clothes to wear
> If things go on I'll die in despair"
> (Rohlehr, 218)

It is to be noted, though, that this anxiety did/does not prevent men and women from living together as families or raising children even if they do it in a visiting relationship.

While there is some merit to Rohlehr's point that economics features in the identities men and women held of themselves and each other, and therefore in the decisions they made (and continue to make) concerning sexual relations between them, the question of ideological resistance cannot be gainsaid. Marriage in and out of calypso was considered a thing for elites, and associated with control and loss of independence for men primarily, but also for women. It is an institution of the state which, under colonialism, is invested in promoting arrant racist domination by the colonizers. Lamming uses marriage as such a trope in two stories in *Castle* told about lower-class conjugal relations.

Lamming establishes early in the text that conjugal forms among the working class are more often than not lacking approval by the state. In a discussion among the boys we learn that most of them are "without fathers," that is, either the father is a visitor to the home of the boy and his mother, or he does not support the child financially (Lamming, *Castle* 46). Then in a discussion between the boys we hear two stories of love intrigue in the relationships of Bambi, Bots and Bambina, and Jon, Susie and Jen. In both these allegorical tales we have one man who is in relationship with two women. In Bambi's case, he also has children from both women, who, by the way, know about each other and are the "best of friends". Bambina's children are Sugar Shine, Turtle Dove and Stumps; and Bots' children are Puss in Boots Number Two, and Suck Me Toe. Jon lives with Susie and they have two children: Po King and Puss in Boots Number One. Then Jon meets Jen. As the children's nick-names clearly intimate, already Lamming, like a calypsonian, is milking these tales for their comedic value.

The crises in the two stories arise when the "thing they call marriage," in one of the boys' words, intervenes (Lamming, *Castle* 141). In Jon's case, he joins a church called the Free for All Brethren and "get save." However, he also begins a relationship with the pastor's daughter, Jen, and impregnates her. The Pastor insists, threatening to shoot Jon dead, that he should marry Jen or else. Jon shares the story with Susie, but gets an unsympathetic response. She argues that if anyone is to get married to him it will be her, if not she "would poison his guts out" (Lamming, *Castle* 123). The long and short of the story is that Jon, fearing death on all sides, promises to marry both women. On the day of the wedding however, he remains undecided between the two and from the top of a tall tree in the cemetery he can see both churches where the two brides arrive to find no bridegroom. Lamming never tells us the outcome of this story and we are left up the tree with a divided Jon while the news spreads around the village. Evidently Lamming, like other kaisonians, has no qualms about scandalizing the little as well as the great.

Bambi's story ends likewise in the cemetery after the notion of marriage enters, but in his case his final indecision is fatal. Bambi actually marries Bots when a white German anthropologist comes to the village advocating that couples living in "sin" (having children without marriage) should do the right thing for their children's sake. Of course she does not offer a solution as to what should be the outcome for children of the woman not chosen; the anthropologist never even discusses this. Bambi takes the matter to the two women. They seem not to have a problem with the outcome since they expect things will go on as before. Bambi spins a coin, heads win, and Bots wins. Then the trouble starts.

Bambi has a massive, unexplainable change of personality and starts drinking heavily, and regularly beating both women. The women themselves start to blame each other for his behaviour and then they too start to fight regularly. Bambi drops down dead one night, but this fuels another round of confrontation. Both women want to bury him and their respective undertakers fight over who will bury his body. In the end neither woman has enough money for the funeral, so it is the state that buries him in a pauper's grave.

There is no doubt that Bambi and Jon become conflicted about choosing one of the women, in Bambi's case even after marriage, and therefore both Bambi and Jon find themselves in a fatal division that lands them both in the cemetery as ultimate losers. Like Zeigfield's calypso quoted above, Lamming's tales warn (men) of entering the state of marriage, which he equates unequivocally with white people. He places the stories within the context of racist cultural domination and goes even further by showing that even for women the consequences of acceding to such domination are not favourable. Freedom and independence for both men and women are equated with the locally authorized conjugal arrangement, while the arrangement of state approved marriage is equated with violence, madness (unexplained behaviours and things going off "pop pop in your head") and/or death (Lamming, *Castle* 142).

Although Lamming rather overstates the argument here, he makes another more profound point. It seems that at the heart of the complex accommodation with history and culture that is represented by the local family arrangement, is a deep uncertainty. Many of the enslaved Africans had come from societies where polygamy was practiced, and no doubt to some degree this practice influenced post-slavery forms. However, even more importantly, the history of slavery, despite resistance by the enslaved, produced fractured family forms which would also have influenced post slavery family forms. Blacks at the lower end of the social system would have been fashioning their family forms out of accommodations made to the various historical influences and to the imperatives of their daily lives. However, these accommodations would have come under the pressure of western cultural imperialism, which validates only Christian marriage, and in the face of this onslaught their uncertainty is revealed as a fatal schizophrenia.

We may also read the presence of the schizophrenia described above in the calypsonian's traditional admonition to men to avoid marriage, while at the same time they uphold it as an estate that improves status. In any event, my claim is that here we see Lamming using the calypsonian's love intrigue tale to articulate a Caribbean allegory about freedom. In his particular restatement of that allegory, freedom is shown to arise only in an ongoing complex negotiation among all concerned parties. If only Bambi had known this, he would not have become an alcoholic spouse abuser whom Lamming has to kill off to make his point.

The Calypsonian/Novelist as Griot

Calypsonian Atilla the Hun sang a calypso *Ode to Russia* in 1943, which illustrates the well-known characterization of the calypsonian as griot, or folk keeper of the people's history (Rohlehr, *Calypso and Society* 349-350). This is a familiar characterisation that many have also given to the early writers of West Indian fiction. Certainly, it can be given to Lamming as his novels all seek to render aspects of Caribbean history, not only of the past, but also of a future he ably predicts. However, it is Lamming's adoption of the pose of calypsonian which gives him access to this title of keeper of the people's history, particularly in respect of the novel *Castle*.

I select Attilla's calypso, *Ode to Russia* for its similarity of socialist sentiment with Lamming's chapter on the 1937 riots in *Castle*, but more so for its formal features of reportage and oral history making. At the time of Atilla's calypso *World War II* was in progress, Trinidadians were finding the presence of the American military in their country less than glamorous, and were singing about it in their songs (Rohlehr, *Calypso and*

Society 345). Calypsonians, Rohlehr tells us, still "continued to select names for their tents" and themes for their calypsos, "that reflected the idea of war" (*Calypso and Society* 346). This was also the period when England and other Western European nations were altering their attitudes towards Russia in the face of Hitler's Nazi threat (Rohlehr, *Calypso and Society* 347). In his song Atilla offered his take on the matter for the community, being sure to critique the British as hypocrites, even though he agreed with their new stance. The formal structures highlight that reciprocity between calypsonian and his immediate neighbourhood to which Lamming referred in an earlier quote.

As oral historian, the calypsonian must find ways to keep his audience focused on and remembering his tale. He must also give them a handle on which to hinge their responses to him. Both these objectives are served by the rhythmic pattern that is achieved by the end rhymes, and by the repetition of certain phrases throughout the song. The steady rhythm of *Ode* gives pleasure to the hearer, while the end line of each stanza, although the wording changes slightly from one stanza to another, signals the arrival of the familiar word "Democracy." This repetition allows the audience to sing along at these points. The calypsonian hails them and they can respond. We note Attila's skilful manipulation of these formal features, and his integration of the speechifier's skills, wit and irony.

> "The stone that the builder rejected
> As a corner stone has been accepted

The Red Army is marching triumphantly
And bringing desolation to Germany
So from being the foe of humanity
Russia is now the friend of Democracy

There were criticisms you can't deny
Of the Russian policy in the days gone by
How many of you can remember still
A book that was written by Winston Churchill
In which by our Prime Minister we were told
Communism was the worst thing in the world
But now he is declaring quite differently
That Russia is the friend of Democracy.

The right wing press was abusive
Their articles were vituperative
For Russia was the home of anarchism
Bloodshed, horror and terrorism
They nearly went mad with indignity
At the non-aggression treaty with Germany
But all their talks was hypocrisy
For Russia is the right hand of Democracy

Whoever thought at the start of the war
That Russia would have been one of the big four
Who met at Teheran just recently
To decide on the world's destiny
I wonder how Churchill and Roosevelt feel
To be fraternizing with the man of steel
For after being criticized so bitterly
Josef Stalin is the Saviour of Democracy

I think and I'm sure you'll agree with me
Very soon there'll be a great Allied victory
And Russia will protect every working man

> During the post war situation
> There'll be no more starvation and pain
> No more millionaires and paupers again
> Wealth will be distributed more equally
> And we'll enjoy what is real true Democracy"
> (qtd. in Rohlehr, 349-350).

Kamau Brathwaite calls the effects achieved by the repetition of theme, improvisatory effects, in his case, the "Jazz riff" (*Jazz* 87). He explains it as "a kind of collective response which marks the end of one improvisation and the beginning of the next" (*Jazz* 87). In the calypso, these effects also inhere in the calypso's dramatic method (*Jazz* 82-83). The Calypsonian makes an elaborate argument in a story that he addresses to his audience directly. He aims to bring his own spin on events that the media and politicians are differently reporting. He brings support for his argument from esoteric sources (Winston Churchill's book), and this is a factor which his audience will especially enjoy, since part of his role is to impress them. He has a concern for grand sounding words which he presents with a certain formality. He strings together words like "vituperative," "anarchism," "indignity," and "fraternizing," all the while accompanying them with creole linguistic constructions where rhyme requires and wit permits.

However, the calypsonian undercuts the words of his calypso and the manner of their presentation with a simultaneous approach that is definitely tongue in cheek. This is signalled at the beginning by his question "How many of you remember still/A book that was written by Winston Churchill." It is more than likely that his audience would never ever have heard of that book, far less read it. He emphasises this tongue in cheek attitude again when at the end he suggests that his audience will agree with his expectation that all poverty, pain and privilege will forever end when the allies with the help and direction of Russia win the war. He and they both know that no such thing will ever happen. But he turns this serious matter into good art for their entertainment.

In respect of *Castle*, we see Lamming performing some of the strategies which Atilla uses. Lamming constructs *Castle* around the theme of the 1930s labour upheavals that constitute a significant period of Caribbean history. These labour struggles span the length of the island chain between the years 1934-1938, and express a spontaneous coalition of peasants and waged workers that rose up to demand better working and living conditions for the poor and working class peoples of the Caribbean. Out of these uprisings sprang the trade union movement and political parties that would propel the countries into independence.

In Lamming's narrative on this history, one should note first that the events of the labour riots in the book are all reported rather than narrated as they happen, and are done so in a predominance of simple sentences, which serve to heighten dramatic tension. Further, the reader should take note that the author gives the role of reporting to two of the village boys, Bob and Trumper, and to the old drunken woman who occupies the fringes of the village social structure (Lamming, *Castle* 194-201).

Lamming, like the calypsonian, wants to represent that first, there is no seamless collective action among the poor in respect of the confrontation, and hence no single voice can suffice either to describe or explain it. The calypsonian and Lamming are fully conscious of the issue of competing narratives and hence authorisation of the meaning of events. In the interview with David Scott in the journal *Small Axe*, Lamming asserts that there always "remains an area for free choice... about the meanings you place on events" (qtd in Scott 123). He recognizes that one could be separated from full understanding of events through the exercise of power and control over language, but argues in effect that if language was an infinite source of control it was also an infinite source of invention. Here we have a theory of the calypso being articulated of which we can begin an account by examining Atilla's *Ode to Russia*.

The calypsonian well recognizes that language, and hence behaviour toward Russia, were being manipulated and ordered by the Western allies. In fact, he ironically draws to our attention that the ultimate state of Western authorisation of the word had been achieved: commitment to script in newspaper and book. However, Atilla tells us that, driven by new exigencies, Churchill and his allies are now "declaring quite differently." Atilla thus feels free to interpret their words in whatever way he chooses, since they are revealed to be dealing in "hypocrisy."

The allied authorities ("powers" in several senses of the term) lose their ability to either proscribe or prescribe meaning and the calypsonian feels free to speculate about their feelings at being forced to eat their words by Russia. More importantly, he seeks to make sure that history will record through his prophesy that Russia, the underdog—a position he knows quite well as one who has been colonised—held the key to "a great Allied victory." In other words, they could say what they wanted, in whatever print they wanted; I Atilla, and you whom I am trying to convince with my alternative evidence and interpretation, will know the real truth about that history. Lamming similarly pronounces with his reporting of the riots.

Just as Atilla feels free to articulate his own account of historic events, so Lamming presents his subjective accounts of the labour uprisings in the city through the subjective reporting by deliberately unofficial raconteurs. He merges the villagers' speculations, the stories of two boys who had gone to see what was happening, and the reactions of an old woman whose son was killed by the riot police, to create historic account.

The second reason that makes Lamming's strategy of using storytelling to report on the riots significant and akin to the calypsonian's, is his fascination with the performance aspects of all these events. The calypsonian has to stand up before an audience and deliver the narrative. While she/he hopes and expects that record sales for the individual's private enjoyment will occur, most if not all songs are produced for the festival stage where singer and audience expect to interact in a communal event. Likewise, the public nature of the events interest Lamming, not the individual's private reflections on the matter. While the novel is a private experience, one may speculate that the author expects the stimulation of a communal reaction to this record of the most important public event of Caribbean history since emancipation. The communal aspect of the report of the riots in the village in Chapter nine of *Castle* is made evident in the busyness of the scene where the reports happen, and the direct address to the reader that is simulated in the dramatic reporting of events by 'eyewitnesses'.

While the villagers are shut up in their individual houses for much of the action, to demonstrate their fear and uncertainty, the author places discussions of the riots in a scene of much coming and going. Mr. Foster goes to the police station and a few persons gather on his step for his news. When they leave and go home, Bob's Father goes over to Mr. Foster's. Then, Pa comes outside for a while and speaks to several of the householders from the street. When he goes in, Bob arrives and his father comes home, only to return a short while after to Mr. Foster's house to get some medicine to revive Bob who has fainted. Then Trumper arrives and speaks a little from the street and returns to his house to be followed by Bob's father. After this, the old woman arrives and several villagers join her on the steps of one house to hear her story. This going back and forth goes on for some time, and then the men from the city arrive to gather in huddled groups near the houses until the Landlord walks up the street. The men follow him at a distance until Mr. Slime arrives. They all leave and the chapter ends with the police driving through the streets, which are finally silent (Lamming, *Castle* 202-208).

Each aspect of the scene is shaped like a mini performance on stage. One just has to imagine this scene being acted to see how it could keep an audience attentive to the stage and caught up in trying to figure out who all the characters are and how they connect to all that is going on. This section, I suggest, is inspired by the theatre and performance of the calypso competition stage. Comments that even Lamming himself offers support this reading.

Lamming's comment in the interview with Scott, when he indicates his fascination with the contradictions being shouted by the crowd outside the Moyne Commission meetings held to evaluate the riots, clearly signals this interest in the performance. To elaborate on that story told earlier, Lamming recalls that the post–riots Moyne Commission investigations were held in Queen's Park, where microphones were set up outside the building so that people heard the questions and answers of those appearing before the Commission. He says, "What I remember very well is the intervention of the crowd shouting, 'That's not true! That's not true!'… That investigation in Queen's Park is an even stronger memory [than the riots themselves.]" (qtd. in Scott 78). His comments underscore the almost choral quality of the crowd's responses to the speakers. Here we note clearly too the concern with the question of authorization that the crowd's responses indicate. These factors seem to influence the strategies the author uses to structure the novel to present the events.

A second factor to note in the chapter is that certain sentences and phrases reoccur at intervals, which replicate the calypsonian's repeated line or chorus. Repeated lines in the novel function just as the repeated lines in the calypso: to anchor the issue being discussed and to serve as a hook line to keep the audience interested and connected to the story. In the first part of the chapter the phrase repeated is "fighting in the city." This is said at least eight times and each time more information is given about the events of the strike. In the second section of the story a chorus is created by two phrases: a woman "started to cry," and "they comin, they comin", the latter said by either Bob or Trumper at various moments in their narratives. In the last section where the repetition is less frequent, similar choral phrases, each repeated three times are, "he couldn't stand it," and "fire the stones." The first is in reference to the villagers' response to seeing the landlord walking along the village road totally terrified by the labour riots. The second phrase refers to cries by the city rioters who had come to the village and were poised with sticks and stones in hand to attack the landlord.

The repetitions enhance the dramatic effect, and lend a musical, rhythmical cadence to the narration. It would not be impossible to put the narration in chapter nine to music and sing it as a calypso. The only thing missing would be rhyme.

A third point to note is that each repetition involves the individual/group tension which Brathwaite says surfaces and is resolved in *Jazz*, and which may also be seen being worked out in the calypso. The first repetition of "fighting in the city" can be seen as the collective assertion of a collective narration. The adult villagers' anxiety about the breakdown of the accustomed social order and their concern that they will be called on to act either for or against it is captured in this repeated phrase. No one in particular is credited with this phrase.

When the narration moves to "started to cry," the phrase is reported to be the act of Bob's mother, or Miss Foster or Bob's mother again. The boy's phrase is also either Bob's or Trumper's. In each case, a single voice is speaking.

In the final two calls, the collective voice returns. In the case of "couldn't stand it," although it is Mr. Foster and Bob's father to whom the words are attributed, they speak a feeling that we are told earlier is the attitude of most if not all the villagers. When the villagers discuss the threat to the landlord they collectively agree, the narrator says, "Whatever happened in the city they didn't want blood to be shed in the village" (Lamming, *Castle* 199). The final repeated phrase about "firing" stones is also a collective call that is the attitude of the unnamed rioters who have come to the village and are trying to urge solidarity for their position. The scene closes with all the villagers shut up inside while a police car with a collective of black men armed against their people prowls menacingly through the streets. However, here again the individual voice returns, as Miss Foster's unspoken thoughts are offered wondering whether she was glad that the rioters had left just moments before the police arrive. The individual/group tension has been resolved and the status quo returned, but as always with an uneasy peace that is only bought through coercion and violence.

5 Gender Relations in Castle

This chapter makes the case for a reading of the women in *Castle* that foregrounds them and recuperates their agency. As such, the critique may be made that it sets out to correct images of the colonised or of women if we read them in the ways this study suggests. The criticism is that in seeking to state what the 'real' woman is like, the writer who points to the fact that women possess agency and power fail to consider that the 'real' is a contested construct; that literature is not simply a reflection of reality but a site of competing 'truths'. In other words, that there could be no one "real" woman (Moi 45-46). However, despite the strong roles that Lamming gives his female characters, he does not leave women or mothers unproblematised. Mothers can be unreasonable or domineering, as sometimes are The Mother and Mrs. Foster. Mothers' relationship to fathers or to sexual partners may also be perceived in terms of their need of men and men's accommodation of them. At least, according to the boys in their discussion on the relative merits of absentee fathers, unequal relations seem to be suggested. And often, through their internalisation of certain colonial values, as is the case of Ma's defence of the Landlord, women can be the staunchest defenders of aspects of the status-quo. Such is the case when Ma fails to criticise economic relations that are critical to continuity of exactly that status quo.

A related criticism may also be that in pursuit of authentic representations, theorists thus concerned with truth dig themselves into a hole of reifying realism as a literary strategy. In other words, any discussion of what women are 'really' like implies that the literature that represents them is necessarily a realist literature that assumes the transparency of literature. But realism is not the only form in which literature can present; consequently, the critique about 'real' women in literature that is not realist is unsustainable. In Lamming's case, although he is very interested in issues of representation he does not hold to the novel as a strictly mimetic device, nor does he hold to realism as his sole literary strategy. If he shows anything, it is that the 'real' woman is complex, both the same and different from official attempts to render her.

The Critical Eye on Gender in *Castle*

A foundational point of this chapter is the need for a re-examination of how critics construct certain gender identities in texts. The post-colonial referential text is a kind of photograph with indexical relations to its subject similar to those of a photograph. The critic then becomes a key mediator on seeing the text. Yet the critical act is left largely unexplored, though it is fundamental to the visual construction of gender in the text.

The argument is persistently made here that it is possible to look at the women in *Castle* from their eyes and how they act in others' talk about them and see not merely victims, and by extension to see Lamming as not necessarily a misogynist writer. Even where it appears that they are being victimised, it is possible to come to the interpretation that Lamming gives his representations of women the agency to choose outside their own interest. In this sense he does not make them simply victims of others, but figures capable of and engaged in constructing the social world they inhabit. In the case of Ma for example, in choosing to retain certain aspects of the colonial status quo, her choice is predicated on a higher choice that locates her outside the whole construct of colonialism in important senses. Is she victim or collaborator? Does all the power indeed reside in the hands of patriarchal Creighton, or absentee fathers, or violent and patriarchal spouses or the overseer class or opportunistic Slime? I think not. Women hold up at least half the sky in Creighton village.

One can argue productively that in many ways, Lamming's orchestration of the carnivalesque in the novel *In the Castle of My Skin* identifies an interest in and an exploration of gender that challenge traditional expositions of this work. Whether he was conscious of this interest or not is immaterial; the evidence of a gender analysis of the text suggests it. Here I borrow Eudine Barriteau's definition of gender to mean "complex systems of personal and social relations through which women and men are socially created and maintained and through which they gain access to, or are allocated status, power and material resources within societies" (Barriteau 2001, 26).

This chapter concentrates mainly on women, but is not limited, as has been done with this text, to finding the things that oppress them either as characters in the text or in the author's orchestration of subject positions by which he invites female readers to imagine themselves as women, or invites male readers to "know" women. As Barriteau's definition says, gender connotes complex systems, and efforts to discover an unvarying voice of doom when it comes to women's lives or some men's artistic engagement with them is a foreclosure on 'truth'. This is a position I think Crudella Forbes, who looks at several other Lamming's texts in *From Nation to Diaspora*, would support.

Nevertheless I am unhappy with what I see as Forbes' uneven and problematic deployment of the concept 'gender'. She sometimes makes fundamental contradictions even in terms of her own definition of it, which includes acceptance of it as a "complex of social relations" (4). For example, despite having said that it refers to social relations, she equates it with biological sex in her reference to a "single" gender (7). She takes an unsafe position also by her inference that gender, this time correctly meaning social relations of gender, is a microcosmic index as opposed to the "macrocosmic" concerns: race, culture and language (Forbes 5-6). On the other hand, Forbes does present evidence that bears out my own findings about traditional expositions of Lamming's fiction, and my propositions about social relations of gender in *Castle*, properly understood.

Forbes tracks deployment of gender in some of the major contributions of particular West Indian men's fiction (including Lamming's work) and concludes, drawing on three important texts of her survey, that the critics believe that these men's fiction serves to further the oppression of women whether by "inadequately represent[ing] women's oppression" or "actively creat[ing] structures of such oppression through their narratology" (2). One of these critical texts from which Forbes quotes in substantiating this conclusion is a 2002 work by Sandra Paquet (2). Paquet's canonical first study of Lamming's novels in 1982, *The Novels of George Lamming*, comments on the gender bias present in these works as Forbes agrees (257).

A more recent reading of *Castle* along the classic lines described is provided by David Williams in the chapter "Rereading Our Classics: *In the Castle of My Skin* and *The Lonely Londoners*" in the book *Gendered Realities: Essays in Caribbean Thought* edited by Patricia Mohammed and published in 2004. Williams makes all the given "discoveries" of Lamming's masculinist treatment of the women in *Castle*: Women are said to be "consistently...

used to evoke the 'sleep' that Lamming presents as the negative condition from which Creighton Village must awaken" (292). Williams distinguishes the character Ma from that of Pa by her deficiencies and his strengths. He shows Ma to be religiously invested in the continuation of the feudal structure of the plantation, having accommodated to it as a good thing, while Pa "is conscious of how exploitation and betrayal have dominated the region's history" and wants to resist it (292). Mrs. Foster is reported as being submissive, G's mother as both authoritarian and powerless (which characteristics, by the way, contradict each other). The drunken old woman, Williams says, is presented as a "derelict" and "nightmarish" "ikon of female existence in the novel" (292). Williams also sees in Lamming's presentation the equation of colonial power and authority with female images. This contradicts his previous assessments of being female. In addition, Williams fails to explore how the feminisation of colonial power and authority impact on his generalised conclusions about how Lamming treats women and power (293).

These typical conclusions that Williams makes about women and gender in *Castle* need re-examination. Women in this text do not always passively endure their circumstances, limit their interests to narrowly defined domestic issues, nor are treated in marginalised or rigidly circumscribed ways. In resolving his artistic dilemmas by turning to solutions present in the vernacular culture, Lamming reveals women in *Castle* in a different way. This difference allows us to imagine that he is neither misogynistic nor otherwise oppressive of women. While Forbes rightly recognises this absence of misogynism in respect of four other Lamming novels, she does not include *Castle* among these (214). Even Dr. Lamming himself, in an interview with this writer (see transcribed interview on page 255), states that he takes up the question of gender from his novel *Seasons of Adventure*, where he says the character Fola is "ahead" of any other woman in *Castle* (10 Aug. 2005). However, I suggest that evidence in the latter novel exposes the limitations of even Dr. Lamming's perspective.

Hearing Women's Voices

If the central character as Lamming says is the community, then one has to see that he makes choices in the text that support the argument that a large indisputable chunk of what constitutes that community are the words, ways, reflections, knowledge and visions of the women of the community. Elaine Fido, in the conversation with Carole Boyce Davies which constitutes the preface to their book (*Out of the Kumbla*), uses the term "womanist" (xii) (which she borrows from Alice Walker) to describe a concern with women's "talk, customs and lore" that can be appropriate to describe what Lamming is doing here. I will show this to be the case, if one is not wedded to a definition of 'concern' or 'interest' which is based on counting numbers of appearances by women, but is based more appropriately on what information is given when they do appear or the quality of that appearance. It also requires one to see interest and concern in terms of what the author effects and not necessarily in terms (or only) of his intentions. What Lamming is able to effect in this novel is indebted to popular culture as a knowledge system; in this knowledge system, women's lives bear re-examination.

Fig. 2: Female revellers participating in
Barbados Grand Kadooment 2002.
Source: http://www.2.justbajan.com/cropover/2002/kadooment/4.html

A factor Lamming could not avoid seeing, and I suggest could not avoid being influenced by, is that women hold significant place in local festivals and other popular cultural performance modes. This includes all the performance forms that Lamming uses in *Castle*: carnival, Landship, savings societies, popular expressions of religion, street theatre like the Pentecostal church street meetings, folktale and folk sayings, calypso or a way of singing hymns which is very like calypso, comic theatre. In these masquerades women and their forms of politics have jostled vigorously for discourse space. We see this especially vividly displayed in the case of the woman in the centre of the photograph in figure 2 above. She interacts with the eye of the camera very directly and thus reveals that she is actively engaged in the process of meaning made from this photograph.

Unfortunately, women's perspectives and hence powers have not always been privileged by particular narrative voices or literary and cultural critics. However, if one observes the mechanisms of narration rather than take the narrator or the narrator's perspective for granted, one can see women appearing in these popular texts and in *Castle* in roles through which they wrest and celebrate power and control, especially over themselves and also on behalf of others. It also means looking at the underground of the text where the so-called minor characters and stories exist.

Curwen Best offers an important way of understanding what is meant here in his tuk theory. He suggests that the initial narrative stance taken by the lead penny-whistle, the 'narrator' in the Bajan tuk band which introduces the theme and supposedly carries the composition's melody, "though important, is not enough to go by." (*Roots to Popular Culture* 62) This is because of the melodic variations, improvisations, transgressions of all the instruments, including the humble 'steel' or triangle. These would have lifted the actual performance, its "freshness and intrigue" (*Roots* 62), into centre stage for admiration, even though the often familiar theme promised a jouissance based on the linear value of the familiar melody. Lamming in *Castle* performs a similar destabilization of narrative function.

In drawing on the practices of orality, Lamming is able to exploit its consequent heterogeneous, and sometimes contradictory, voices. He stresses storytelling and changes of narrator with consequent fragmentation. The narrator is sometimes G, sometimes an omniscient third person, sometimes characters in their own voices as given in straight dialogue of a play. To both make denser his drawing of the world down below, and to present a critique of colonial education, he includes local popular sayings and songs like the ones taught to the children in school to help them memorise information:

> "Thirty days hath September,
> April, June and November;
> All the rest have thirty-one
> Except February which hath but twenty-eight
> and twenty-nine in a Leap Year." (*Castle* 41)

and:

> "a b   ab   catch a crab
> g o   go   let it go
> a b   ab   catch a crab
> g o   go   let it go." (*Castle* 40)

While both of these can be read in the derisory tone that critiques the education system as has been done, both of them also have very practical and useful functions in the text that validate popular culture. The first is a jingle in Barbados that helps one to get easily to the memory of how many days are in each month. This practice is still utilised even by educated adults as I know from my own use of this mnemonic device. The second is a good Bajan way that calls on the children's cultural life, in order to teach them to understand the concept of syllables to aid spelling. In other words, it uses popular culture to aid Standard English language acquisition. Failure to account for this meaning is to deny dialogization in this particular tale in the text. One needs to bear these oral double voices in mind to better understand how women's gender roles play out.

Lamming does not follow neatly the Aristotelian narrative structure of a chronologically ordered text with a beginning, middle and end. He breaks up his text with a dream sequence. He presents a whole chapter (chapter 4) and parts of others as the dialogue one would see in a play. He even includes a detailed recipe for making the Bajan national dish, cuckoo (*Castle* 274).

The advantages to Lamming's use of orality as counter-discourse are several. Most importantly, it enables multi-vocality through shifts in linguistic register, and consequently opens out the power of authorising or taking authority. Multiple discourses are made evident through these different 'languages', not all of which are in the control of dominant forces. This offers the possibility of seeing how the oppressed must accept some responsibility for their state, and consequently, how they control some degree of freedom to change their circumstances. In other words, they are not statically portrayed as victims. This is the case with the women in the novel. That critics have been able to see women only in disempowered ways in this novel reveals the way that critical projects themselves insert unequal relations of gender in the world of this text. They do this when they fail to account for the multiplicity of stories and perspectives present in it. It has been possible for critical explorations to produce unitary readings of such a dense and heavily populated text with its multitude of socio-linguistic worlds, and this is very telling. It signals to us the still to be adequately explored relationship between critic and the text, especially when it comes to analyses that purport to treat with gender relations in novels of the West Indies.

Women can be observed in *Castle* constructing worlds and histories out of and against the challenging circumstances available, including but not limited to patriarchy. If the voices of dominant masculinity, officialdom, high seriousness and linear trajectories are privileged in reading *Castle* or the other texts on which it draws, women can indeed appear as passive, boxed into narrow definitions of the domestic and therefore as the objects of power only. We see women being assessed this way by Carole Boyce Davies in her chapter on Caribbean proverbs, folktales, folksongs and the calypso in the landmark text on Caribbean women and literature (165-193).

Boyce Davies concludes, though from somewhat skewed evidence, that treatment of women in oral literature is predominantly negative and characterizes women by lack of integrity and heroism (185). However, if we privilege women's own voices in the oral text and bring to the centre the spaces and strategies they engage, we are forced to question these conclusions. This is the strategy we can then apply to evaluating women in *Castle*.

In the institution of the folk narrative in the Caribbean, the construction of women on the surface appears 'outlawish' and vociferous. Anxieties at the heart of tendencies towards race, class and patriarchal domination attempt to demonise this behaviour and either characterize such agency and vociferousness as undesirable or seek to invert, pacify or otherwise deny it. However, the narrative itself acts as a record of the other voice. There is not only another voice of struggle, that is, of evidence of another desire, that voice often signifies overcoming, or desire realised. The challenge is to observe the existence of the paradox for a more accurate reading of social reality. To do otherwise is to privilege a hegemonic voice, to follow the penny-whistle, which seeks to affirm a monologue. Unfortunately, the latter happens even in the case of readings which aim to champion women against patriarchal domination, like Boyce Davies' reading. The following is an example.

Boyce Davies admits that the line of the folksong "Woman is a Nation grumble too much" does indicate "solidity and empowerment" and speaks of "a structured female political sphere." (165) However, she manages to cancel this out by concluding that the final words "grumble too much" make "clear" the "subordination" of women (165). While it may be true as she argues that a tendency to put a woman in her place can be inferred from this line, a tendency for women to resist being silenced can also be inferred. One just has to keep in mind all the information in the line rather than accompany its linear trajectory. What this line does make clear is that the social order is a divided "nation", and people who give themselves the freedom to grumble (or are likely to) in the minds of others who evidently do not want grumbling to happen, get songs sung about them and their behaviour. To conclude that this subordinates them is either a leap of faith that takes the perspective of the lead narrative voice in the line, or it is a defeatist fear that patriarchy is finalized and absolute, when in fact it is a tendency that may be successfully overcome as much as it can oppress.

The interests of all in the society are not safely reconciled. The line records social conflict and poses the question of order as one of power relations where power does not reside in the hegemon alone. Analytical conclusions made of the oral text are more appropriate therefore when they are about how power is defined, engaged and resisted, and not about the women's actual victim status, or men's victor status for that matter. Dependence on the narrative voice or a straight non-ironical interpretation of that voice in the oral culture is not always advisable. This is particularly true when one recognizes that the assumption, generally un-stated but nevertheless held, that the folk texts are all created by men or from a man's perspective may not in fact be true.

A look at several of the folk songs in the book, *Folk Songs of*

Barbados by Marshall, McGeary and Thompson and the book, *De Mortar-pestle: A Collection of Barbadian Proverbs* by G. Addinton Forde reveal several interesting features of gender relations different from the ones Boyce Davies proposes. Lamming exploits several similar features in *Castle*.

It is noteworthy that in *Folk Songs*, which covers a very wide range of folk songs sung in Barbados, over half mention or otherwise focus on women. Many also privilege the female speaking voice. Even in the section entitled "Songs About Men" (which contains 10 songs to the 17 in the section about women) half of the songs recorded deal with women's effect on or treatment of men. Read according to Boyce Davies, several of these songs infer a desire to discursively construct the image of the evil woman or the poor victimized woman (165). However, read another way, one can see the insistence by women on making decisions about their lives; one can see them enjoying power and demonstrating personal heroism and integrity. Alternatively, one can also see men enduring passivity as well as being evil in the worst way, depending on whose values the hearer privileges. This is frequently seen on the question of sex and sexuality, a source of commentary in many of the songs.

Women Exercising Choice and Power

In the song *Panama Man* (Marshall et al 61) the persona may be perceived as money hungry and materialistic when she refuses to be courted by the returning immigrant who has come back penniless. She says, "But 'e cahn get me wid-out de money to buy me a taffeta dress." (61) This is an interpretation made explicitly by several male calypsonians and critics of this type of song, as Davis shows (174-185). However, it raises the question of whose interests are being served by such an interpretation. What is never explored in this perspective is that the woman is both expressing desire as a sexual being and that she is setting the terms of sexual engagement. These are equally valid interpretations of that type of song.

Furthermore, the song *Panama Man* also removes so-called "love" from its bourgeois conception as an unencumbered disembodied state in which no relations of power, exchange, negotiation and materiality are engaged. The absence of such relations in love relationships is the unspoken assumption of the "money-hungry materialistic" critique. This is the lesson that Bambino, Bots and Bambi come up against in *Castle*, and their failure to recognize that they had already worked out a balance of these factors in their "good live wid" leads to the literal break up of their working conjugal arrangement by a bad marriage.

Bambino's death is interrelated with the fact he asserts power as a patriarch over the women, whereas before the marriage, the threesome existed with the very real permission of the two women involved and the shared material responsibility of all. It is true that the man has two women, but this in itself is insufficient to assert that patriarchy exists. The existence of traditional patriarchal relations prior to this is undermined by the fact that Bambino finds it necessary to consult the women on the matter about entering the new arrangement of marriage with one of them. In their agreement to the new arrangement the women exercise choice/power. They could have both said no and threatened, like Jen, to poison out his guts. Patriarchy is realized only when the man starts to beat the women, and he is killed off by the author. The death sets a clear statement in this novel about love and patriarchy which does not support an idea of Lamming being misogynistic or oppressive of women in his portrayals of women's images, certainly not in this novel.

Additionally, in the world down below and the world of this song, everyone is allowed to be interested in sex, even the poor and penniless, the man and the woman. The returning well-off immigrant in the song, the Curaçao man whose wealth is symbolized in the calico dress that he could provide (Marshall et al 62), the Panama Man with only his "Spanish Caress", and the woman who evidently had both of them, all are legitimately free sexual beings. The words of the song seem also interested in ridiculing the inability to make the most of one's opportunities, which has its negative consequences, in this case inability to get some.

Panama, to Barbadians of the period 1850 to 1914, represented upward mobility for the class of workers who went off to help build or work around the Panama Canal. Lamming himself makes reference to these workers in *Castle*. Interestingly, he includes women as a category among them. As the authors of *Folksongs* support, many of these workers remitted considerable sums for the upkeep of their families and to save to purchase real property that would enable them to have a better life upon return (Marshall et al 61). It was no small matter therefore for a Panama man to return penniless, for which his inability to buy a taffeta dress is a metaphor. The song records, though it does not go into the reasons why, that this real history of some returning penniless existed. It would have been a caution to those entertaining undertaking such a popular venture.

However, the question of the woman wanting material objects to this man's self-assuredly legitimate 'non-material' request still needs to be explained. Again, one should turn to the circumstances to aid interpretation and this may suggest doubts about the non-materiality of the man's interests as well as supply support for the equal legitimacy of the woman's response.

In the circumstances of the times, if not now also, 'love' generally meant and means responsibilities of children and someplace to put them. Responsibilities also included validating one's status as an adult and as a member of a community by demonstration of some improvement in personal circumstances. This was the case for the socially well off as it was a case for those down below. It also applied to working class men despite the much touted stereotype of the irresponsible saga boy or village ram which is the principal representation of Afro-Caribbean man.

Although popular culture recognized this saga boy type, it also represented a man as a responsible being. An example is the Barbadian proverb which equated the definition of manhood with responsibility: "Evah man yuh sih in a shirt an pants en' neider man," which meant do not expect all men to behave in a responsible manner (Addinton Forde 27). This proverb identifies that some men do not fit the definition, but it equally establishes that the standard is the responsible man. Another more pertinent example is one a rural respondent told me to explain that he was now sharing a house with a woman for the first time and buying household furnishings (Wayne Waldrond 24 09 94). He said the villagers would tell him he was "sleeping man sleep," a saying that means demonstrating ability to mind the responsibilities of sexuality.

On the part of women 'love' also inferred responsibilities for home and children. It is a well established fact that the working class woman helped/helps provide for family and household living expenses in the Caribbean.

With regard to care of children, though women often face even more hostile economic circumstances than men, given their lower employment levels (Gill, *Women, Work and Development* 22), most do not refuse to mind the children once they have them and do whatever they can (Gill, *Women, Work and Development* 19). Everyone, the woman included, takes for granted that children 'belong' to a woman, and significantly, that they represent resource and power for her as much as responsibility and liability. Children also belong to a woman as source of affective support, and as a resource when they get big enough to help around the house and in a woman's old age. Therefore, when faced with the request to 'love', especially in the hard economic times of this song, women knew the proverb "Wha' sweeten goat mout does bun e' tail" (Forde 8).

Sex in the 'money for things' songs is frequently associated with the necessity to demonstrate resourcefulness on the part of the man. The woman must be equally canny since she cannot be naïve about the future. The woman in *Panama Man* evidently has no doubts that the burdensome material consequences of sex are at least a possibility. She explains her denial in more detail by fleshing out what the man is really asking for. She says, "If de Panama man gwine court wid me,/He gwine treat me like a queen." Another song says, "If yah wan' ta live in sin, /Get a lil' house an' put me in" (Marshall, et al 11).

Perhaps hidden in the accusation that this is a 'material girl' and that this somehow demeans womanhood is the unspoken demand for womanhood to be sexually acquiescent as well as ignorant of the full ramifications of how material life permeates sexuality in the existing scheme of things. Perhaps this is the predicament that puts Jon in *Castle* literally up a tree when he bites off more than he can chew by getting a woman pregnant while he is involved with another. Death threatens him whether he marries the one or the other. He is evidently incapable of satisfying all his responsibilities and leaving him up a tree is one indictment by the author on Jen's patriarchal demands and assumptions.

This 'love' then, is not disembodied or free of the terms of the material life for either partner. However, if we look to the value put on sex by everyone, then we see that the penniless Panama Man was also dealing in another kind of materiality. The nesting instinct associated with women often implies the nurturing of those in the nest, though not always as songs about lazy women indicate, such as in the song "Weh Muh Jenny Gone" in Marshall McGeary and Thompson (90-91). Even if all the woman gains from the exchange with this man is a "Spanish Caress", the man also gains indirectly in having his reputation and his capacity to attract some woman's care enhanced. Recall, all are allowed to be interested in sex. Use of the term "Spanish caress" to describe what he is offering establishes the pleasurable nature of sex and hints at some capability, even of an exotic nature, on his part. In other words, his material stock is also increased.

He would also have gained in another way, for it is the woman who owns/controls sex in this genre of song and he would have just got it for virtually nothing. One Barbadian folksong puts it, "Wha Dovie got um is all she own" (Marshall McGeary and Thompson 11). She is the dispenser of this commodity that is desired by all, and she attempts to use it to get the best consequences for herself or at her own discretion. However, what is never discussed is the interest on the man's part in the sex for things songs in manipulating things or worse in order to achieve the victory of getting it for nothing. The man too is seeking his own interests. In some cases he is often apparently willing even to represent that interest by abuse and use of force. In the last song quoted which is called King Ja Ja, the man responds to Dovie's negotiating position with, "But if yuh wan' to play the fool,/ah get a big stick an' Ah keep yuh cool" (Marshall McGeary and Thompson 11). Evidently, domestic violence is an un-reprimanded option for some men. Mind you, it also is for some women as one Bajan folksong indicates. In this song the female persona sings, "Ah ent kill nabody but muh husband, so ah kin face de judge independent" (Marshall McGeary and Thompson 6-7).

What then about Boyce Davies' accusation of un-extended credit for heroism and integrity towards women that marks folksongs? Even in the genre of song selected so far, it is possible to talk of women's integrity if we mean by that their honesty and self-respect. Nor do we have to go further to discover their heroism if by that we mean their courage, boldness or daring. Unless the critic is himself or herself using the terms of bourgeois respectability which organize the world to support unequal and untruthful relations of domination, then the woman's heroism and integrity are not difficult to see. She names the relations of sexual exchange for what they really are. She dares to express desires that are unsanctioned for women by embracing sexuality, and she dares also to want stability and a level of material comforts that other categories of people seem to want to enjoy as of exclusive and natural right, but deny the same to her.

A reading of the line of "Woman is a nation" by Boyce Davis supports this evidence of the nation women's integrity and heroism. They ask for what they want in the face of evident opposition; thereby they demonstrate the courage of their conviction. They express their own desires according to their own schemes of legitimatization, their own truths that enable expression, even if these are different from those prevailing.

Even sayings that are said to demonstrate their deceitfulness such as those Boyce Davies lists (169), can expose women's or the particular woman's possession of these more positive attributes of integrity and heroism if you privilege the woman's voice in the saying and return the saying to its context. For example, unless you want to suggest that the woman should always dance when asked (or have sex or do any other thing that she evidently does not want to) then you recognize a woman who is true to her own desires and daring enough to voice a strategy that she believes would ensure that desire is effected in the world by whatever means. In the Jamaican saying, "Woman no wan fe dance him say him frock short" (169) is an example. Another saying Boyce Davies selects for this list, "woman two face like star apple" (169), can be similarly read if we return it to context and we listen to the so-called silent woman rather than the speaker. It may just as correctly be deduced that these sayings also point to an organization of power or normative structures that do not facilitate a woman saying exactly what she thinks, as that she is not a teller of the truth.

The point here is not to present women as unfailingly heroic or their acts as inevitably having integrity. It is to enable the ascription of integrity and heroism to embrace what the woman or women in the particular saying do in the context of relations of power and in the context of a fuller rendering of the socio-economic circumstances. The point is also to challenge the tendency of critics to silence women's full engagement with their humanity, including their own assessments and self judgments. Truth is evidently being established as a contested site in the examples given. In the terms of the tuk band theory, improvisation and variation by other instruments challenge the penny whistle's attempt to establish one melodic truth. To read these examples as evidence of women's victim status or of the consistently negative portrayal of women is for the critic to foreclose that contest. Foreclosure is disallowed by the principle of the grotesque and carnival laughter that dethrone and reinstall with full interest in reinstating equality. This is nowhere else most present than in respect of women in popular festival activities of the West Indies, where women 'out' their 'grotesque' bodies in the marketplace.

Newspaper records of women and festivals show that women have always constituted a particular figure of concern for official culture. Gordon Rohlehr quotes from nineteenth century newspaper records which report on the significance of women's presence in the Trinidad carnival (*Calypso and Society*

213). These newspaper reports make several references to the 'obscene' dancing and 'profane' singing of women on the streets at carnival. These women, Rohlehr reminds us, "then, as now, were the focal point of much moralising commentary" (*Calypso and Society* 213). The phenomenon of the female masquerader/ street performer has deepened in recent years, to the extent that women now form three quarters or more of the carnival and Barbados crop over masqueraders.

In respect of the Landship and the phenomena of savings institutions, research still has to be done, but anecdotal evidence suggests that from as far back as the 1920s women were a significant force in these bodies. In respect of pictorial evidence, women can now be seen to constitute the majority of Landship performers. They have also played other roles in these festival activities. Women constitute significant and growing numbers of the persons participating in Crop Over as band leaders, costume designers, producers and as back-up singers for calypsonians. More recently, their numbers are increasing as calypso artistes in the junior and adult categories, and there is at least one tent manager. Therefore, the woman is a force we must consider in any investigation of culture that draws on or represents festival modes, such as does Lamming's novel *Castle*. Furthermore, we must be aware not only of how others perceive them, we must be equally concerned about how they see themselves. It is only in attending to both perspectives that we can accurately conclude about women's place in social relations.

Given Lamming's stated intention in *Castle* to constitute a testimony to the civic relevance of the 'people' of the world down below and of their valid human experiences, it is important for this study to attend his treatment of women qua women in his text. In other words, women are automatically an important focus given that they are unequivocally dwellers of that world 'down below', if by down below one means not only subordinated class position but also the place of those who the dominant culture would marginalise and exclude generally from privilege and certain kinds of power positions.

Mothers, Spouses, Old Women

Admittedly, Lamming locates motherhood as a site of social control where patriarchy is reproduced. While noting that it can be a source of women's oppression, a critical site of their subordination as we hear in the boys' talk about mothers, Lamming interrogates it as a source of power. In this he is not far from the position taken by some black women novelists and theorists.

The stereotype of the mother is one of the stereotypes of black women against which black female author/theorists inveigh. In southern United States and the Caribbean, as a strategy of slavery, the black woman was the one perceived as the mother, the 'mammy'. Black theorist Barbara Christian argues that stereotyping black women as the mammy allowed white women to participate in the congruent stereotype of the pure, innocent, fragile, ornamental romantic female figure (Christian 2). The stereotype that was promulgated by both white and early black writers, presents the mammy figure as grossly fat, nurturing, fanatically religious, kind and strong in the sense that she herself needs or demands little (Christian 2).

It is true that Lamming does articulate some of the stereotypes about mothers/spouses. In another story in the novel he has the character Trumper declaring in an uncontested way that once a woman gets a man to marry her, "you can't sort of get 'bout as you like, an' the woman always seem to think she's got some special kind of claim on you, as if you're a kind of pigeon or a fowl" (Lamming, *Castle* 142). Women may or may not hold these attitudes to men, and they may or may not be invested in trying to get men to marry them. However, it can be argued that the women in both these stereotypes are attempting to exercise power. If they do not succeed it will not be, apparently, for lack of trying.

Lamming also marks mothering as a space where women can achieve personal power even when they appear as foil to a main character. (I use the traditional term 'main character' here to refer to the character G, though I see Lamming's point that the real 'protagonist' is the village and its inhabitants. I however contest the designations of 'main' and 'minor' characters as well as the concept of 'protagonist' which carry concepts of class distinction into critical practice.)

Although we never get G's mother's name, The Mother in *Castle*, like other women in the text, stands as a figure of strength, agency and resistance, and this is not only conveyed in her name or authoritarian behaviour towards G. The story in *Castle* is the boy G's among others, but The Mother is right there at the beginning of the story. She is the one holding the important key to the boy's past and his connections to family and community through her control of memory.

The Mother is very much like Pa, the old man, in respect of giving place of importance to history. Just as Lamming gives him the key to the African past that he resurrects in his dreams, so The Mother has the capacity to provide meaning to the self through her control of memory of the West Indian past in her memoirs told to G. And in her recounting of the family history in response to her boy's queries, it is significant that she states that the grandmother went to Panama to work in the construction of the Canal. Formal historiographies have yet to document the history of West Indian women who migrated to Panama during the period of the great West Indian migrations to the Canal Zone. Histories have been focussed on the migrations of men during this period (See Velma Newton's *The Silver Men*). However, here we have Lamming throwing up this important but neglected piece of Caribbean history from the voice of a woman. He does little with it beyond this mention, but the mere record is important. The woman who offers it offers more than just family history, she offers community history. She is engaging history as a discourse and demonstrating how the oral culture manages this important personal/family/community resource.

Mothers, then, exist squarely in the officially unsanctioned oral culture in this text, and Lamming, like many other West Indian writers, sees this culture as a realm of being and knowing of great counter-discursive possibility. Women, particularly mothers, are linked with the culture as transmitters of orality, and male and female West Indian writers exploit the oral culture as a site where a distinctive counter-culture against colonialism is upheld and celebrated. The oral culture represents the splitting off of what is not doable or say-able in official culture. This is not to say that it is a binary opposite of the official; too much interplay and potential for interplay between the two exists in social relations. But oral culture is present within the individual as a fund from which erupts contentious mores. It is significant, therefore, that women are the spiritual guides in this realm in *Castle*.

However, the trope of the 'mother' works in a complex way in West Indian literature. Male and female protagonists are forced to see the mother in a dual fashion. She must be defined as in some ways collaborating in her own oppression (as her apparent acceptance of colonial religion and her problematic relation to child-father testifies), in which case the protagonist separates from her as a necessary loss to enable maturation. On the other hand, the mother, or the culture she represents/which represents her, must be re-envisioned and reintegrated into the psyche to be carried forward as a strategy of counter-discourse.

The boy G goes through his parting from The Mother at the end of the novel; however, his interior monologue in the very last lines of the novel, and Lamming's formal presentation of it, is testimony to the other vision of the re-integrated counter-discursive mother: "The village/my mother/a boy among the boys/a man who knew his people won't feel alone/to be a different kind of creature" (Lamming, *Castle* 303). Rendered as lines from a poem but kept together in a single line, the arrangement places the word 'mother' inside the text and also makes it integral to the metaphor of "a different kind of creature". The reading is that the boy must keep them all and the way each contributes to the other together in his memory: village, mother, equal boys, the knowing of one's people. This knowledge will enable and empower him to be other than the official images of himself presently available to him. The sound of the penny whistle, in other words, is improvised on and the resulting composition is a 'different kind' of song.

The man the boy G is going to become will not be powerless; rather, he will be immeasurably empowered to be creative and independent if he is able to integrate The Mother among other significant aspects of his former life into his repertoire of memories/skills.

Lamming also undermines the colonial and patriarchal complex in the name of motherhood by expanding the roles mothers perform vis-à-vis that complex. When Mrs. Foster goes to the Landlord to get him to undertake his custodial role of fixing things after the flood, he takes the position of superior and sees her as supplicant. However, she takes as a right his responsibility for reparation after the flood. Therefore, she quite boldly makes the positive step to go to him and invoke his responsibility rather than passively await his decision to act. He gives her a pittance, but he also serves her tea with a tea-cup and saucer just like he does his friends who visit on the housetop. Can one not speculate that this points to his confusion at her bold move to come unsolicited to invoke her right to have him be concerned about her loss of house from the flood? If it is just his demonstration of control by dispensation of favour, she does not take it so. True, she appears to enact aspects of the colonised role which has internalised self-abasement when she is so uncritical of the Landlord's definition of their relative status, but I have earlier offered another ironic reading of this which destabilises such an interpretation. She installs the discourse of reparations in that not so simple action of requesting something that should ordinarily have been his to concern himself about, rather than hers to ask after.

We again see the mother undermining the colonial patriarchal complex in the case of the drunken old woman who goes to the city during the riots to find her son and returns to report to the villagers. Her son's death by the riot police weighs heavily, yet she takes time to also sharply criticize Mr. Foster and the village men for not participating in the riots. "I jus from the city...

while you a big stinkin' nigger man wrap up in yuh blasted bed. I been in the city an 'tis men like you they want" (Lamming, *Castle* 197). The role of organiser that she takes in this speech is all the more significant, in that she represents a figure that is so at odds with what is considered proper not only in terms of colonial manners, but also of the way that patriarchy would have women behave.

Apart from mothers, other women who can be seen as mother figures play roles that are self-directed and self-authorised. Ma, as we have seen, is one such woman. In reading her role, it is important to understand that the community sees her and not just her husband as a leader. In her interaction with the villagers who go to buy bread at the bread cart they give way and leave her a clear pathway ahead of them. She takes that privilege as her right. More importantly, Ma is the only one who raises concern when Pa and the villagers would equate Mr. Slime, the ex-school teacher, with his seemingly radical plans, with the Biblical Moses who delivers his people from their oppressors. She recommends that the village take a more sagacious look at Mr. Slime. Mr. Slime, in fact, betrays the whole village by literally selling them out and Ma's caution proves prophetic.

Ma rejects Mr. Slime against her knowledge and interpretation of the Mosaic liberator model. In the Biblical model, the position Moses takes that makes him leader is self-sacrifice (Exod. 2. 11-15, Exod. 3. 1-10). Moses takes an ultimate act of solidarity with his enslaved peoples upon seeing an act of abuse by the

Egyptian slavers, by killing the Egyptians involved. However, his action alienates any possibility of his continuing to enjoy privilege as the adopted grandson of the Egyptian Pharoah.

Ma correctly reads that there is nothing similarly self-sacrificing about Mr. Slime's promotion of the Penny Bank and Friendly Society. She stops just short of actually proposing that a more appropriate model to understand Slime would be that of Judas, who takes care of the money for Christ and his disciples, and who is understood as having been corrupted by that role. Judas and Slime can be seen as models of the capitalist corporation, whose interests are impelled by individualist profit motives. Their interests coincide with the interests of the people only in so far as the former can be realised through the manipulation of the latter. As Preston Melville brought to my attention (02-07-2005), one can look for a detailed exploration of this model to C. L. R. James' text, *Mariners, Renegades and Castaways: The Story of Herman Melville and the World We Live In*, which asserts that the model of the corporation is exemplified in Herman Melville's Ahab and the ship Pequod in *Moby Dick*.

Another mother character that Lamming utilises to produce alternative readings of the villagers' circumstances is the old woman who gives the true story about Barbados' slave past to the boys. She is held in stark contrast to the teachers of authorised history at the school, that site of imperial control. They would have the boys forget their true past; however, that is a forgetting that leaves them with no authentic sense of the self.

It is reasonable to speculate that she has told this to a school child, but even if she has not she seems to have identified roles for herself as a recorder of history, of the truth, and a dispenser of that truth and history. It is unlikely that she is unaware that colonial schooling is disseminating a contradictory history. But even if she were, consider the implications of her tale that places her and her kind in a relationship of extreme exploitation and oppression vis-à-vis Mr. Creighton and his kind. It is not possible for that tale not to politicise the people even if they were unreflective of their current circumstances before hearing it. If she were just engaging in gossip, in spreading such a tale, her gossip is not idle and without import in the world she inhabits. Whether the listeners of her tale take the next step and use the information she supplies to liberate themselves is another issue. By being a voice of truth of the real relations that bind Mr. Creighton and his friends and family, the school inspector, and the people of Belville to the villagers, she has struck a blow for liberation against the colonial patriarchal complex.

Women of the Official Class

What of the women of the official class? Are they victims or evil, passive or authoritarian? And are these their only options? The young Ms. Creighton may dress the part and accompany her father on his "show of arms" charade on Sundays, but she is busy sexually transgressing the Miranda code out of sight of her parents. Or by her choice to be silent when she is almost discovered, she secures that code, no doubt seduced by the privileges it offers as much as she is cowed by its power. Her mother also dresses the part on Sundays and at rooftop teas, but she is also often sick. This makes inter-textual gestures to Jean Rhys' *Wide Sargasso Sea* and the madwoman Bertha/Antoinette. The value in 'madness' is that it allows alternative constructions of the self that challenge what official culture or any other orthodoxy permits. The headmaster's wife, we recognise, takes her own way even as far as reversing roles with the patriarch—she beats him rather than the other way around.

None of these women of the official class appear asleep, though they may all be in need of an awakening. However, what they need to awaken to is no different from what all the men need to awaken to, as well as all the women and children of the world down below—the egalitarian vision of a just society where negotiation of difference and power happens and can lead to equal dignity for all.

Conclusion: Art Interrogating Life, Theorising Experience: A Dialogue with George Lamming

This study began with the observation that is by now taken for granted: that West Indian literature is a hybrid form; by that I mean far more than the participation of the novel *In the Castle of My Skin* in two poles—traditional scribed literature and vernacular oral forms. This novel participates in art not only as political polemic, but also as comedy with its attendant knowledge constructions and performances. *Castle* participates in creating theory and creating artifact, that is, the art form the novel. It signifies as poetry and also as prose fiction. It manipulates the artifact/novel as word and the artifact as sensible figure or visual shape of word on the page. These features qualify this novel for consideration as a new form of literary expression that is apparently very uniquely West Indian. This is a central conclusion to be presented in this final chapter.

A second conclusion is that from as far as the first novel *Castle*, Lamming foregrounds a political role for aesthetics. Thirdly, a fruitful area for further research lies in pursuing a link between the absence of critical exploration of popular influences on the West Indian novel and West Indian people's disconnection from it. A final conclusion is that gender analysis of the West Indian cannon can identify new links between aesthetics and transformation through broadening the terms of what transformation means for West Indian society. I present those conclusions partly as a dialogue with the author's responses from the two interviews conducted with him. The transcribed taped interview is presented as an appendix to this study.

Castle's newness in respect of boundary crossings should disturb practice in how we study West Indian novels as it has resonance with other West Indian texts. Jean Rhys' *Wide Sargasso Sea*, with its disruption of narrative function and destabilization of narrative processes, is a case in point. Traditional narrative aspects 'normally' enable us to recognize who is important and who is not to a text's development, but these texts open the sphere of such considerations. For example, Rhys narrates *Sargasso* from the perspectives of both Antoinette and her English husband when we may by habit see Antoinette as 'protagonist' and her husband as 'antagonist', and have this signaled to us by a more nuanced entry into her motivations than his through the function of narrator. With the husband narrating his own perspective, he cannot be exempted from consideration as a quite significant centre of construction, energy and sympathetic evaluation for that novel. In that sense, he participates in whatever is that centering role that is normally known as 'protagonist'. That term might need replacing with one that is not so heavily invested in a problematic binary construction, and might lead to other ways of analyzing literature of the anti-colonial period.

Kamau Brathwaite's developing use of font size and video symbol to consolidate and disseminate meaning as he does in his Sycorax video style is another example of this newness in dispersing narrative authority. It is possible to correlate what Brathwaite does with Lamming's creation of a matrix for the rhyme "a-bab, catch a crab" which the boys sing for the inspector's visit, and with his presentation in the form of poetry presented as prose of G's struggle for understanding in his indirect speech at the end of the novel. These developments suggest that we have hybridism in a way that extends the usual meaning of the term. Hybridism here means crossing boundaries of artistic genre rather than just merely between literary genres. That is, here there is crossing from the literary into the visual. We are meant not just to read the text, but to see how type is being manipulated and thus consider its significance to meaning.

The implication of the above is that along with the need for a whole new terminology to talk about West Indian literature, we may need to understand in a more nuanced way the political role given to popular aesthetics when they appear in texts. The notion that literature does political work is not unfamiliar to Marxist literary theory, and it is reaffirmed in this study of Lamming's *Castle*. In interviews Lamming articulates this recognition (see interview in *Small Axe* 112). Indeed, through *Castle* he demonstrates this theory by his treatment of popular culture. It is to see that in this treatment Lamming's textualisation of vernacular forms enable them to impact on the reflective processes termed 'civilization' itself, of which the written text is a valuable expression. Exploration of West Indian literature could be immeasurably enhanced by recognition of the influence by West Indian popular culture.

Derek Walcott asserts in a poem that in the Caribbean, "the sea is history" (25). If by "sea" we also understand a metaphor for the ubiquitous common culture, Walcott could have also added that it is philosophy. The carnival, popular festival arts and the ideologies that inform these arts, share these roles of encoding West Indian history and philosophy. The carnivalesque inscribes itself in the formation of West Indian 'nation states' and civilisation, and in the literature that signals and promotes, as well as interrogates the evolution of those 'states' and that civilisation. *Castle* harnesses oral popular culture strategies as literary mechanisms towards political ends. These strategies allow Lamming to generate new knowledges about Caribbean society; to proffer new modes of perception; to produce a new language to help assess, critique and transform Caribbean political economy. As he reveals in the appended interview, Lamming brings this principle to fruition in his attempts both to return the history of working class people to them via the theatre (his 1980 work with the Barbados Workers Union), and in the calls he makes to produce Caribbean literature as feature films (Lamming, 10 Aug. 2005).

Lamming's sentiment from the Scott interview that our politics is central to our aesthetics (112) is reiterated by him in many ways in the appended interview. He points out that in his novel *Season of Adventure*, the fourth in the series of six works, he specifically locates aesthetics at the heart of his attempt to represent existing political struggles about what kind of state would serve Caribbean societies best (Lamming, 10 Aug. 2005). In *Season* Lamming chooses a band of steel pan players to bring down the republic. The novel also ends with a little girl being taught to play the pan—a signal of where the future of that state will/ought to evolve in respect of the imperative of making popular visions central to the formation of the state and the processes of governance. However, Lamming seems to suggest that *Season* is the first time that he works through political issues centering culture as a vehicle or epistemological tool in his novels. This study concludes otherwise.

In one test of the hypothesis that even from the first novel Lamming was influenced by carnival and calypso in particular, he was asked in the interview which is appended to speak of his involvement in carnival culture in Trinidad during the time he lived there and prior to the production of *In the Castle of My Skin*. He reported that he attended carnival tents to listen to the calypso competitions, and while he never donned a costume, he would make certain to be on the streets for both Jour Vert and the street masquerades. When coupled with the fact that while in Trinidad and before he wrote *Castle* Lamming was part of the group of intellectuals who were exploring popular cultural motifs like the carnival, pan and other folk practices as the basis of a national identity, this strong personal interest in carnival as a cultural practice suggests that the recognition of carnival as a political metaphor cannot help but have been already germinating in the earlier book.

Admittedly, Lamming does assert in the appended interview that "carnival was inconceivable in Barbados at the time [period of the late 1930s, which is represented in *Castle*]" (Aug. 10 2005). Burrowes, on the contrary, points to the appropriation and carnivalising of British maritime uniforms by Landship members, and their combination of these with music and street pageantry in spectacle and festival play during the 1930s (228). As historian Aviston Downes also records, the friendly society was also a significant feature of organization (Downes, "Sailing" 101; Downes, "Discerning Sense 1). Having grown up in Carrington's Village, the home of what was during the early 1930s the largest Landship and Friendly Society in Barbados, Lamming would have been drawing on his knowledge of these phenomena when he placed the Friendly Society that Mr. Slime organises in *Castle*.

Lamming is fully convinced of the political role of the land ship and believes their membership had a very self–conscious political thrust. In the interview with the author he makes reference to the proposition made to him in England by a Barbadian scholar, Peter Blackman, that the Landship was a reconstruction of Marcus Garvey's Black Star Line on land (Lamming, 10 Aug. 2005). Blackman based his evidence, Lamming says, on the fact that many of the Landship members were Garveyites, and that many of the people behind the 1937 riots were Garveyites. Historians have spoken little of this link, perhaps because they place the beginnings of the Landship back in the 19th century (Burrowes 219-220; Downes 93); however, Burrowes records that when Garvey visited Barbados in 1937 many land ship companies formed part of the official welcoming committee. At his first engagement at Liberty Hall, she says, "24 men and women dressed in the uniform of the Barbados Landship 'York'... formed a Guard through which [Garvey] passed while the African National Anthem was played on a Coronet" (226). This Garvey/Landship connection, though disjunctive in time in terms of the origins of each movement, is still a rich vein of scholarship worth pursuing.

While Lamming did not directly utilise the Landship in *Castle*, his placement of one of its primary organisational strategies— the Friendly Society—at the center of the text, establishes metonymic connections with the society's subversive carnival associations and connotations.

It is important to understand these contextual influences since the author makes referentiality an important aspect of his mode of presentation. This makes the author's extra-fictional ideas such as offered here in these interviews important sites—though not the only sources—of meaning in the fiction. This might contradict the concept of authorial fallacy which suggests that the author is not the authority of meaning in the text. However, to give the author some control over meaning asserts that the author 'is people too' as the Layne-Clarke character contends, and is thereby worthy of being kept alive as opposed to pronouncing/effecting his/her death.

As Clement Ball rightly acknowledges, two of the chief distinguishing features of the discourse of postcolonialism are oppositionality and referentiality (2). This does not mean that the work is a 'mere' mimetic or realist representation of the world (Ball 2), just as realism is not the mode (or more correctly, the only mode) of representing/producing the world in the carnival and other types of popular culture. Like the carnival satire that it models, Lamming's text is aimed at some transformative purpose in a historical reality. This recognition also ought not to automatically suggest that oppositionality is a deficient maneuver because it keeps the imperial force always on stage. Oppositionality illuminates structures of domination by flowing out of and through its cracks and fissures like a dye introduced in a system to trace abnormalities in functioning. By so doing, it clarifies the two forces—domination and opposition—as parts of a single system that both offer information for system transformation.

We cannot deny that the very textuality of the satiric work, like the popular culture performance and the maneuvers Lamming effects in *Castle*, weakens its possibilities for bringing about change, as some critics argue (Ball 34). After all, the text cannot literally sanction the subjects that it targets. However, it can alter consciousness of some readers towards the change(s) it envisages. This consciousness can then be mobilised by persons or groups to effect change. I propose that it is after this fashion that popular festival arts of the West Indies offer new ways of envisaging society—as a social formation where equality and freedom are necessary and possible—that may initiate or accomplish change. By raiding this culture for his models, Lamming further disseminates the accompanying carnival ideologies about equality and freedom. He argues in one part of the interview for a new language by social engineers, a "new mode of perception," which can more adequately and justly serve the society (Lamming, 10 Aug 2005). His work in its fullness is aimed at bringing such a language with its new modes of consciousness into existence.

A third conclusion of this study is that the disconnection of Caribbean people (at home and in the diaspora) from the West Indian book may well be the result of the failure of critical practice to demonstrate how integral to this book are West Indian people's popular forms of reflection and theorizing. The assumption here that people want or need this literature could very well be a middle class belief about the importance of what has become an essentially bourgeois cultural product, although to be fair to Dr. Lamming, he may very well be talking only about integrating the different worlds of the society by bringing book and popular culture together. He could be suggesting that the people do not have the option of refusing the novel because they do not otherwise get its peculiar structures of knowledge and explorations of ontology which is also their heritage. We do know that if the people want the novel, they could possess it through the very carnivals they have created. The models exist where masquerade leaders, acting in that domain of mediation that Lamming spoke of, explore colonial texts of European and Caribbean history, the Bible, American movies, Caribbean folklore and other sources for ideas and images to present as masquerade themes.

The preference for calypso and other popular narratives over the Caribbean novel may well be because the former allow more democratic participation in these signifying oppositional structures, and hence in the creation of history. Julia Kristeva makes the relevant observation in support of Bakhtin's carnivalisation theory, that "History and morality are written and read within the infrastructure of texts" (36). Transcendent notions of philosophy and power are also there written; hence, the question about disconnection can be read differently. It may well be: Why is calypso not used in understanding West Indian novels? Similarly: Why could calypso, or Crop Over, or the Landship to give a few examples, not be texts through which students at the university level could be taught philosophy, economics, history or the law? In other words, it is not only that official texts can offer something to the people; the people's unofficial texts can offer something to the reading and epistemological practices of officialdom.

The fourth conclusion is that through its carnivalised structures, *Castle* supports the view that culture performs the role of transformation. Lamming is ambivalent in *Castle* as in our interviews. Although he argues in the interview following that it is perhaps only in culture that interventions to transform Caribbean society will arise, he argues that transformation is presently off the agenda in Caribbean society (Lamming, 10 Aug. 2005). He believes that culture is being reduced to music in the Caribbean, but in his words, "a music that is very anti-intellectual" (Lamming, 10 Aug. 2005). He notes too that many Caribbean music artistes are being seduced by being promoted internationally without their apparent recognition that many of the injurious colonial expectations as in previous times continue to obtain (Lamming, 10 Aug. 2005).

Some cultural theorists will argue with him about the nature of much of certain aspects of dance hall music (see Carolyn Cooper in *Noises in the Blood: Orality, Gender and the Vulgar Body of Jamaican Popular Culture* and "Lyrical Gun: Metaphor and Role Play in Jamaican Dancehall Culture"; or Natasha Barnes in "Dancehall Lyricism"). In addition, it may be shown that many calypsos, even the ones thought to be 'merely' party music, continue to keep to an original characteristic of the calypso, its sustained concern with social critique and hence with transformation, and that Dr. Lamming in his dismissal of the present music culture is obscuring this. However, that discussion is beyond the boundaries of this study. What is more relevant to this discussion of the transformative capacity of *Castle*, which result as **a consequence of its carnival borrowings** is his assertion that transformation is off the books.

There is no denying the existence of an on-going struggle by many Caribbean women and some men to transform gender relations in Caribbean society. This current opposition to patriarchal domination is revealing the deeply flawed nature of the development of Caribbean civilization as much after political decolonization as before it. By searching out how women achieve, express and struggle for agency in this text, analysis made in this study is a self-conscious part of that effort of transformation given identification by this author as a feminist and activist in the arenas of culture, political economy, mental health, Christianity and trade unionism. Transformation is certainly still very much on the agenda of some groups and persons in the society and we are taking every opportunity to keep our agendas on the table.

Some may argue that the Caribbean feminist struggle may not reflect the degree of popular representation required for either system liberation/system transformation, or Dr. Lamming's view of what is necessary for such. Nevertheless, this struggle has provided an important conceptual vocabulary and offered important perspectives of other lived realities—that of many women's and other disadvantaged groups such as calypsonians and dance hall artistes for instance—that further interrogate post-independence Caribbean civilization and identity. Sylvia Wynter's analysis provides an important installment in this direction. (See "Afterword: 'Beyond Miranda's Meanings: Un/silencing the 'Demonic Ground' of Caliban's 'Woman,'" of the collection of critical essays on Caribbean literature written by Caribbean women 355-372).

The value of the interventions described above is their elucidation of regulatory and normalising mechanisms that maintain power structures and power relations. Wigmoore Francis explores such regulatory and normalising mechanisms in respect of women in his article, "Nineteenth-and Early-Twentieth Century Perspectives on Women in the Discourses of Radical Black Caribbean Men" (116-139). Not least of these power relations are the ones uncovered by this study's uncharacteristic examination of characters not normally examined, or examined only in relation to a discourse of sub-ordination. This refers to the regulatory and normalizing mechanism of established critical traditions, and the hegemony of certain critical positions that are inimical to freedom and creativity in critical practice and to the mediation of West Indian literature in the continuing project of emancipation. This elucidation offers knowledge important for further struggle in many arenas, not all of which are textual.

Dr. Lamming recognises the importance of women in Caribbean history and civilisation. While he does not use the term 'patriarchy', he acknowledges the role of power relations in gender relations which aim at negating or submerging women's importance (Lamming, 10 Aug. 2005). He also notes women's resistance to this in that world of down below in which this work *Castle* is centred. Nonetheless, in identifying a problem of the dominance of male power in the organisation of social relations and manipulating his female characters to analyse and comment on this, he sees it as an issue that he deals with increasingly from one novel to the next (Lamming, 10 Aug. 2005). He argues in our interviews that in *Season*, his fourth novel, he deals more consciously with the issue of female power and the problems of power for women through the character Fola, than he does with any woman in *Castle* (Lamming, 10 Aug. 2005). He knows what he does consciously, but that concern can be shown to exist from as early as *Castle* when one looks at the women in *Castle* on their own recognizance.

Even if he is unaware of this, Lamming powerfully demonstrates in this text how gender ideologies are created and how gender expresses itself as a social construct, rather than an essence males and females bring to being. Lamming raises questions of gender identity that illuminate the power relations behind identity formation in very conscious ways.

In his use of the popular text in *Castle*, Lamming exploits the feature where the woman breaks free as a subject even in that text's very act of envisioning of her as a disciplined object. Ironically, this envisioning already accepts her refusal to be contained and her right not to be so. Women in *Castle* refuse containment whether in spheres of sexuality, leadership, or economic independence. They reformulate terms of accepted politics, religion, and social space. Often they do capitulate to social forces in order to negotiate their own survival and that of their children, and that leads their occupation of the imaginary, the spiritual realm, in an ambivalent way at times.

One of the ways liberal, radical and socialist mainstream feminisms have stated the argument in terms of women's liberation is in terms of a public private divide, with the crux of women's problems residing in being allocated to the private space. Patricia Hill Collins, Afro-American feminist critic, argues that this model does not fit black women's experiences of family or work in racist societies (46). This model implies liberation for women if they are able to work in the public sphere and gain the economic independence which having one's own money brings or exploitation if they remain within the private sphere of the family and household. However, for Black women in racist societies home is often the source of support and regeneration, while work is experienced as alienated labour and is often the site of greater oppression and fragmentation (Hill Collins, 48). This is not to suggest that home is invariably a positive site for black women in even these racist societies. The experience of oppression of many black women within black homes led Chandra Mohanty and Biddy

Martin to conclude that home is "an illusion of coherence and safety based on exclusion of specific histories of oppression and resistance" (qtd. in Davies, 65).

Lamming, like Hill Collins, refuses to accept that the household is a space that only disempowers women or that it necessarily is in opposition to women's participation in the public space. In the interview following, he supports this conclusion by his statement that the women in the texts are usually "in charge of something... very much responsible for survival" (Lamming, 10 Aug. 2005). He theorises this as the woman being "the patriarch of a household, rather than the object of a patriarch or the victim of a patriarch as such" (Lamming, 10 Aug. 2005). In fact, he asserts, the woman is often the "father" of a house (Lamming, 10 Aug. 2005). The terminology he uses might on the surface suggest that Dr. Lamming accepts some roles as peculiar to men and others to women. He does appear to be suggesting that being the 'mother' of a house has nothing to do with responsibility for household and family survival as a matter of course. However, taking a different view, one can also argue that he accords fully with the feminist position that gender, which among other things expresses as allocation of social roles like mother and father to women and men respectively, is a social rather than biological construct. Thus, women can transcend this structuring and express any role, regardless of gender ascriptions. In other words, a woman can be a father.

Lamming also refuses to separate creation of the public world from the workings and space of the household when he puts the working class household at the centre of national politics. Having centered women in this world of house and family, he thus includes them in the larger political process, in both practical and ideological terms as we see with the riots and the alternative education network.

An important difference between feminist approaches of this study and statements by Dr. Lamming in the following interview needs explanation. He suggests that it was not useful to appropriate mainstream western feminist thought to interrogate relations of gender in West Indian literature. He saw this as participating in the race for theory which is a phenomenon he describes as reflective of a civilization at the end of its generative capabilities, while Caribbean civilization is at the beginning of an epoch and needs a more grounded mode of analysis.

While sympathetic with his call for modes of analysis to be grounded, I challenge his assumptions about western mainstream feminist thought. Such thought is itself a beginning that challenges old and tired modes of western thought. In its central proposition that the personal is political, mainstream feminist thought, in which I can claim to participate, advances western thought beyond any conceptions of being as simply consciousness. It also goes beyond the proposition that material relations are responsible for consciousness and therefore being. This foundational feminist formulation lays bare the power relations inherent in identity formation. The principle that the personal is political must mean that the self is constituted by the ideological and the material and social relations that give rise to ideology, all this while itself being grounded in the material body that eats, belches, farts and dances in the carnival.

With regard to the consideration of relevance, Dr. Lamming fails to appreciate that Western feminist thought was influenced significantly by the conceptions of decolonisation arising from the colonial world. Bill Schwartz makes the argument about the impact of West Indian intellectual thought on British and European thinking that can easily be transferred to movements in feminist thought. He argues that the West Indian search in the West Indian novel.

> "...to devise a form in which the indigenous popular voices of the Caribbean could be articulated... [that is to] confront the question of British civilization... not only as a matter of the formal exterior culture but as a matter of the self, was to understand the intricacy of the interrelations between a civilization and political power. Or more radically, **it marked the recognition that civilization, the symbolic ordering of human life, is power. [And that] in the British case,... there barely existed a conceptual vocabulary in which such a critique could be expressed. Yet we can discern a group of [West Indian texts] which, in their different idioms, attempted to create a language in which just such insights could be deployed.**" (252-253). (emphasis added).

It is possible to argue that Euro-American feminist thought was similarly affected. Certainly, the relationship between Lamming and Simone deBeauvoir, an acknowledged foremother of western mainstream feminist thought, is worth studying. This concept of civilisation being a matter also of the self is essentially what is meant by the conception that the personal is political, or if you wish in this case, that the political is personal. That is, that the large, the macro, the collective is the intimately personal. It points to the power dynamics present in the construction of subjectivity, civilization, 'literature', critical praxis and the individual 'un-literatured' text.

Dr. Lamming's notion of Caribbean woman as expressed in our interviews appears somewhat essentialist: she appears to be the peasant woman who is a single head of household (10 Aug. 2005). On the other hand, it cannot be denied that he also formulates the possibility of a different kind of woman in Cutsie, the black female driver, and even in the landlord's daughter. And if one is unhappy that all these locate women in terms of sexuality, then he offers 'alternative' women in Ma, Mrs. Foster, the drunk old woman, the old woman who tells of slavery, and Mrs. Creighton.

In the interview Dr. Lamming introduced several ideas that bear greater investigation than is possible in this work. Some of these are: his suggestions about the connections between the Landship and the Garvey movement; his notion that the present music culture is following a similar pattern of colonial expectations as existed in the region around the movement of the Caribbean writers abroad to publish in the 1950s; his observations about the change of leadership by race of the new Pentecostal evangelicals in Barbados (10 Aug. 2005); his insistence on the need for a closer look at not only the link between the people and middle class leadership, but also at the inherited political systems. In respect of the latter, as Ball puts it, he makes a judgment not only "of mimic [men's] imperfect or too zealous achievement of colonialist models, but also [of] the choice of models [:] authoritarian models of government, greed, corruption, divide and rule sectarianism, abuse of natural resources and disrespect for common people's needs in the first place." (38) Although these issues are not critical to this thesis, they are mentioned, and the entire interview is reproduced here, as these are nevertheless tangential to the topics pursued in this analysis of *Castle*.

Appendix

Taped Conversation With Dr. George Lamming

10 August, 2005

MG: In all of this work I am concentrating on *In the Castle of My Skin*.

GL: I wanted to ask about that. I read your piece in the Barriteau anthology (Gill, "Feminist Literary Theories") and if you want to talk about gender in the novels, the treatment of women follow an extension. Fola in Seasons is an archetypal figure that is further ahead of any other woman in *Castle*. Millett and the other Euro-American feminists whose theories you use are dealing with a different phenomenon. Woman in the context of Caribbean plantation society is a very different phenomenon. When Millett looks at literature in the European context she looks at [the works of Norman] Mailer and Mailer is very extreme kind of misogynist in his treatment of characters. That is a very different world from our world.

First of all, the world of the Euro American feminist in the fiction is largely a middle class world. It is a world of the white Anglo-Saxon bourgeoisie. The world of the woman, the major figures of Caribbean literature, is poles away from that. She is quite often from down below, and she is quite often the father of a house. That is something that they (the Euro-Americans) could not be dealing in. They deal with separation and divorce and so on. This woman is operating in a very different context of family altogether. She may have a sense of extended family but she is really quite often the patriarch of a house rather than the object of a patriarch or the victim of a patriarch as such. So I would have reservations about how I refer to the feminist theorists of Europe and America. They are dealing with their own terrain.

MG: My major reason for using that approach that I did is as a critique of what I see happening in the Literature programme of Cave Hill. I don't know how they do it at Mona, but I think all of them do it as I see from their readings. How it proceeds is this: it claims works like yours and the early writers for a canon and then because they claim them as canononical works, they approach these works by men the same way as the mainstream feminists approach the male Euro-American canon. I say, you cannot hold these two literatures in the same light. Because a lot of the struggles and responses that are being done in the so-called Caribbean canon are things that the mainstream feminists are concerned about, I see how we can claim your writing for feminist positions and not as patriarchal literature. But I agree with you about the different world of the Caribbean woman character.

GL: There are features in all of the writers of the female characters that lend themselves to a sort of feminist critique of mysogynism. In nearly all the Caribbean women characters there is another dimension. They are usually women in charge of something. They are usually very much responsible for survival.

But in reading Caribbean feminist I see that what starts out as an alternative way of seeing becomes almost a cult. People deal with gender almost as though there is a special cult called gender. Gender is just another social relation, in the way that class is a social relation; in the way that race is a social relation, a social construct. So when one elevates gender into a mystique that can only be shared by, or shared incompletely by and so on, I think that in a way one is just building another kind of cage in which you get locked in. It also does not make much sense to me unless it is men speaking to speak of woman, because that covers a great diversity of individual responses. You will get women whose behaviour could be described as feminist but has no relation whatsoever to some woman who calls herself feminist on a whole range of matters. There is too much flexibility of response to situations and people and so on to have one bracket. Where I think it is true to have the one bracket is if the place of gender as a social relation is seen as very central to a major political struggle, the major political struggle involving gender, in which gender may have to assume an avant guard role; that is, dealing with the dominance of male power in the organization of social relations. Whether those relationships are in the workplace or in the domestic environment, there is an overarching problem of power and hierarchy of which, whatever her class or her background, the woman has a battle of trying to dismantle that dominance. The overwhelming majority of men are not particularly critical of the negative effects of that dominance (male dominance) on the total society.

MG: But I wouldn't say that is a critique one can make of your work. Your work does not address that issue of a woman having that kind of a problem to deal with, of having no power within the household or the workplace.

GL: The later novel, Seasons [elaborates on] this. That is Fola's battle with that world in which she is. It is also extreme. It is then taken up as it never was before in Natives of my Persons, [with] the battle of lady of the house; although that ends in a way that the feminist critics, who do very good critiques of that, don't like. They don't like how it ends. Feminists don't like a woman going back to the man that she should have left. That is completely out of the question (laughs). And she does in a curious way return, and that for them undermines the whole process. Up to there she is doing everything that they think she should do. That again is an area of feeling which you cannot schematise. And she herself says why she does. Some of these too are made in lecture statements.

The weight of much gender affirmation is sometimes very restricting. The truth is that the liberation of women in a society depends very much on the liberation of men in the society. You can't have a society—there is no society—in which you could have liberated women and unliberated men. It is very much like Lincoln and having to deal with [American society] in 1865. You simply can't have a society that is half free and half slave. It can't work. So a society in which women are liberated but men are not, is a society that is extremely explosive. Because every male delinquent is kind of a time bomb, that disturbs the total society in some kind of way. While the liberation of total society is dependent on the liberation of women and it is possible to argue that because historically and in almost nearly all the known societies that the male has been located in that hierarchal position of being in charge of, imagining being in charge of, living the role of being in charge of, the male will not voluntarily surrender that role and therefore in the political liberation of that society, it is very likely that a female force will have to be the vanguard force. [The reason for this is], one cannot expect men to surrender their power in the name of democratizing the society. They will find all ways of democratizing the society provided there could be retention of that kind of economic or power base. In that sense I would agree that there is a very special role women have to play in dismantling that dominance, and a role which men cannot be expected to play in the sense of initiating it. I think there are many men who will identify with women, but the initiatives for it will not come from that end. That is the hurdle which I find, the two things which I find restricting sometimes in the feminist movement: of not seeing that it is the total liberation of the society that is required, and that would mean the liberation of the men as well, with of course the women playing an almost avant guard role. The other thing that you have that the Europeans don't deal with very much when they are dealing with the male and the female, is the tremendous social divide.

In England and certainly with de Bouvoir in France, the feminist movement makes no appeal to working class women. Working class women do not join in anything with French bourgeois women in anything dealing with men. In the context of Caribbean plantation society, and the plantation legacy is still very persistent, particularly in a place like Barbados, the common difficulties that women may experience in relation to men do not at all reduce the social distance between women. You have women who occupy social locations distinct from other women who are victimised by women through those social locations. Although they may be having the same kind of trouble with men, it is not a thing that they will share when one is mistress and one is domestic. That is an important social divide and I am not aware of women making any great effort to bridge that.

So the battle remains a man/woman battle, but the battle is more than [that], the battle is how you bridge the social distance between you and the woman who is working for you. And that is where we get back to where the gender theory is seen as an instrument of class analysis. Then you get a more total and rounded conception of what you are looking at, if the literature is in some way a reflection of the society, of the kinds of tension within the society. This is the general position on gender and how one reads something that is called gender and gender theory. I don't know how you are going to get out of it but I get very uncomfortable too about Caribbean critics getting too caught up in the critical theory position. I think I've mentioned this; people have gone to theory because they are at the dead end of a civilization. The Americas are at the beginning, in a way a prehistory and its coming to an end. We don't really know [how but] there has to be some alternative kind of world because the one we're in is certainly not liveable. It is operating and is on the verge of all kinds of explosions. It certainly can't work by the legacy of these theories that come from people who are reflecting on the end of something.

MG: I am making the case for *Castle* because I see it as a peculiar moment in literature and Caribbean thought, and I wanted to make my analysis around that. I agree with you that I might have to look to the other books to bring some comparisons about what is happening. But I don't want to do a lot of that. I am looking at *Castle* to see what it has to say. I think it has been analysed along with the other books too easily. I think it needs to be pulled out.

GL: It is very different from any of the other books, not only in terms of my other books but from other books in the Caribbean. I mean it originates in Barbados but it actually takes in the whole region. It deals with the whole aetiology of plantation society, so that it connects, whether you are in Jamaica [or anywhere else] it connects. In that sense it has a kind of resonance that may not be so easily found in some of the novels of the same period.

Although that would not have been thought at the time it has what could be thought of [as] a post-modern configuration. It demands a critical approach that cannot be the critical approach to the novel because it is not a novel in the way the novel is a novel. It breaks all the rules of a novel. All the chapters are constructed as though they were stanzas or series of one dramatic poem. So if you look at the form of *Castle*, nearly all the genres are engaged: it has the descriptive narrative of the novel; it converts very quickly into theatre, straight dramatic dialogue without any intervention; it goes into diaries; it goes into long interior monologues. It moves across a great variety and it retains—which was picked up by some people when they were talking about character— the central character as the village.

[The central character] is not the narrator, nor the mother. Everything proceeds from there, comes back to there. The central character is not a person, it is a collectivity. That is also unusual and would give the orthodox critic some problems in trying to analyse character. There are presences in the book rather than character in the formal sense. And the presence is constituted as a collective. *Castle* lends itself to a certain kind of Marxist analysis and you have got that. Kenneth Ramchand is saying really that that is not the emphasis of it at all for him. What for him is the emphasis is the search. What he means is the exchange, the tension which is explored between the narrator and Trumper about this "my people". The irony is that Trumper the unschooled one is very clear about this, but the narrator who is highly schooled would like to be clear but cannot really identify with something he is not clear about. This Ramchand finds one of the major themes, the one that he explores rather than the social layers and the confrontation with the plantation. Where Do I belong? And in a way [G] is left on that when Trumper comes back.

MG: It is so far down the novel that I don't know whether I would say that it is a central theme.

GL: It is far down but it is linked. The narrator experiences [the understanding of class] when he changes schools. My main interest was in how one became a Marxist, the journey. I am explaining that in this way because I didn't discover the meaning of class through [Karl] Marx. I lived class early when I went from one school to another. I was confronted daily with whom I spoke to. The mother in *Castle* has a large area of her ambition [about moving up around her son]. She would not say to her son that he is not to mix with [those] around him, but there is a daily protective thing about where he is and where he is means that he is not with them. They are very conscious of his not being able to join them. There is that negotiating this social distance, although there is absolutely no change in their material circumstances.

Your material circumstances may not change, but your social location may change and create all kind of confusions for you and for others. So the 'who are my people' is really the maturing of the earlier deformation of about where should I go, where should I sit which would have started earlier. So [it] might seem late but it comes out of [something] that is pretty early established between that narrator and those boys.

It may have changed but in my time the school was the major agent of social stratification in Barbados. Very often they were really not good schools. It had to do with scarcity also. There were very few of the things they called high schools. You got in there on scholarship. Poor people didn't get in there at all. They made education scarce and therefore it got associated with certain kinds of privileges.

MG: I argue that in *Castle* you validate an oral history, [placing this next to what is happening in the education system]. I saw an interview with you and Vic Brewster on Errol Barrow where you made the point that you were educated about class by where you lived. The living gave you the history, the social analysis. And I see the same thing happening in *Castle*. The school does not teach history, but history is talked [rehearsed] by the people. There is the old woman who remembers something about slavery and passes it on and all the people get to hear it.

GL: Yes. There are different kinds of history, and the novel is one. I was talking to a French man and I wanted to know what he thought would give a good comprehensive idea of the 19th century social history of France and he paused and said "Balzac." And I said yes, I am aware of [Honore de] Balzac, but I mean history. And he paused a long time and then he said, "Balzac." I then caught on. He meant there is no [French] history like Balzac. And then what he was really getting at was that the fundamental history that is caught is the history of the peoples' feelings. How is that society feeling and behaving? And that is where the oral thing, if you knew how to get it, comes in. The oral thing is sometimes your most important archive. The problem with that is that we have never trusted the oral as a reliable archive. They are getting there. One of [Hilary] Beckles' real contributions is that he probably insisted on orality as an important archive. I don't think that the people before Beckles at [U.W.I.] Cave Hill would have played with that, and that's why we don't have any proper reconstruction of 1937. None of them went out to talk to the people who were alive and around and directly involved. Most of them are dead now. So all of that you have to get from grand children.

On the question of the calypso, this was not any part of the folk or people's music [of Barbados] of that period unless you use [a different definition]. There is this big argument going on now about how you define calypso. Trevor Marshall and some others brought out a book of folk songs [in Barbados]. But Barbados had such a strong ascetic protestant background. It doesn't have that background of the very strong African retentions of Jamaica. In rural Jamaica the African background is very strong—Myal, both the music and the dance. That is what [Rex] Nettleford picked up and did with the National Dance Theatre [of Jamaica]. The Barbados [of that time] is very rigid protestant with very little interventions from other forces compared again with the very cosmopolitan Trinidad. Even the white people [in Barbados] had [that Protestantism]. The first time I heard the Merry Men [musical band of Barbados], which was in Jamaica, what I was very conscious of is that they came out of a hymn background. But it was not the rhythm of Trinidad music or the African thing of a Jamaica music. It was a stylised kind of hymn. If you listen to the old records of the Merry Men you can hear [there] is a hymn tune behind it. Barbadians were all singing hymns. The hymn was their work song. They sang hymns while they were washing and so on. So the calypso doesn't come up in there.

MG: But didn't Trinidad also influence you? You write *Castle* when you are in Trinidad.

GL: No, not in Trinidad. *Castle* is both recall and invention and all of it is written in England. What would happen is that it would be memory filtered through a lot of other experiences outside of Barbados and [even] outside of Trinidad. A lot of the exchange about Trinidad may have had to do with having lived there afterwards and then looking back at it and how it was perceived by Barbados. That [statement about the perception of Trinidad by Barbados] was pretty accurate. Trinidad was seen as a wild place. One had to be very careful about Trinidad. The carnival at that time was inconceivable in Barbados. They tried it once and it didn't come off.

MG: Did you attend calypso tents while you were there?

GL: Oh yes! I went to tents, but more than tents, the carnival event that I was very interested in was the jour'vert. I used to go to the bottom end of Woodford Square, [Port of Spain Trinidad] because there were two or three bands that would pass there. One went behind the railings by the church. For some reason jour'vert had a lot of devil bands, people covered with grease, and they would look for somebody in clean clothes [to rub their greased bodies against you]. There is something too about jour 'vert that had a freshness, an immediacy. Because when they came the next day they were in a sense performing for on-lookers. In jour'vert you were performing for yourself. I never jumped but I had friends who jumped.

There were some people who wore the same costume every year as though that was their trade mark. The thing about that carnival—1946, 1948—is that it would have violence. It would be a big clash of bands. If Desperados ran into Tokyo they had war. If you listened to those names of those bands there was war. That led to a very famous road march by Kitchener, "The Road make to Walk on Carnival Day" I may be dealing with it [in my books] but Lovelace in *The Dragon Can't Dance* actually records the fighting.

MG: Two final things. Why did you choose to highlight pan in *Seasons of Adventure*?

GL: The origin of *Seasons* comes out of the visit to Haiti and really the Haitian drums played at the ceremony of souls. The houngan and the tonelle and so on, that is straight Haiti, but it's the steel pans that take over from the Haitian drums. The theme running through that is the overthrow of the first independent republic. The books follow in that way. The boys in *Castle* are the men in *Immigrants*. The immigrants follow in *Of Age* with the return of shepherd; then *Seasons* follows, *Natives of My Person* in the very last stages of the colonial regime. *Seasons* is the very first chapter of independence in which the republic is overthrown. The point is that the republic is not overthrown by an opposition party; it is overthrown by the drums. It is the bands that overthrow the republic. The point I am getting at there is that the cultural movement is the foundation of political struggle. It is not a political opposition. It is when the bands mobilise the people when the threat to stop them [operating] arises. And of course it is one of the drummers that kills the president. That is the [book] in which the whole theme of the inseparability of politics and culture is most sharply affirmed. That ends on the grounds that while everything is collapsing the one thing that remains is Gort teaching the little girl the drums.

There's one thing I wanted to return to. There was a Landship around in [Carrington's Village]. There is something [else] that I discovered long after. There was a remarkable scholar, a Barbadian called Peter Blackman who left in the 1930s. He became a clergyman and then left the church and became a communist. He was one of the first people I ever met who was doing research in African history in London. He grew up in St. John, just next to Codrington College. He left thirty years and never came back to Barbados. We were once discussing the Landship and he was telling me that what he thought the Landship was doing was reconstructing Garvey's Black Star Liner on land. There was a direct connection because [in] that period many of the landship people were Garveyites, many of the people behind the 1937 riots were Garveyites! That thing of the ship on land was the Star Line.

What confirmed [Blackman's thesis about the Landship being a reconstruction of the Black Starline] for me was that (I did not realise) when the authorities were going to ban the Landship, it was that they sensed that there was some political thrust in the Landship. It connects very much with what Blackman was saying about the Black Star Line. I got this from H. A. Vaughn, a magistrate at the time who was also a research historian. Vaughn told me an interesting story that he was on the bench at the time and they were receiving instructions about severe penalties against the Landship because they wanted to wipe them out. But they were forced not to, [though] not by the landship. When word that the people on the bench, that would be the Chief Justice and so on, were going to get rid of the Landship the merchants intervened. This then gave me the idea in Natives, where the Chief source of authority for the ships is above the House of Trade and Justice. The merchants intervened because they wanted to make it clear that the law was not going to interfere with their trade. You see if you ban the Landship, all that calico and the pumps and so on it would definitely be putting a brake on the sale of cloth, so the law had to retreat. Trade decided what would be just in this situation. The merchants had the review reversed when they calculated what it would mean to what was happening on Broad Street [Bridgetown].

MG: Why did the people not have some kind of a collective response to Slime's betrayal? At the end of *Castle* everyone is individualised. Everybody seems scattered; everybody is now unhoused and individualised.

GL: Slime represents what happens in 1937. People use the name Adams in relation to 1937. But Adams has nothing to do with 1937. What happens is that '37 made Adams. If you look at the Moyne Commission investigations, Adams is always right there. You know when he was approached for the case of Clement Payne he refused the first time. My view is [that the change in him comes from] what happens in the magistrates' court the morning of the same trial.

In that Coleridge Street yard [Bridgetown] there was between 700 and 900 people congregated in a Barbadian courtyard. And he saw his constituency. It was about that crowd. Adams' career is then to some extent facilitated by the Colonial Office as the kind of person who would be the right kind of leader for that sort of movement.

C. L. R. James had a great affection and admiration for Adams which is seen as very odd in the sense that politically Adams is seen as having nothing in common with James. But James' point is that when you consider what Adams is dealing with, they had got rid of Payne but then Adams went into a confrontation with the planter merchant class.

In Barbados at that time if you look around it is a small and very conservative black middle class. So Adams is really out there on his own. There are people who would go ahead from the back, but not out front. There are one or two people like Crawford would be out front and Dan Blackett. But what you would call the Barbados professional middle class is not taking that chance at that stage.

In a way Adams could be seen as assuming a role that ordinary people didn't take on. He had much to do, and [stood] to lose much. He is one of the only politicians known to have played that role in Caribbean politics. Without making one penny out of it! Adams died a poor man. He got nothing in that material sense. All he probably had to live on was the federal pension that they had to argue for. He never engaged in money deals; there is nothing to show of that.

But about the betrayal of the movement of '37—that was a genuine working class movement of down below confronting the state; the parallel in Trinidad would be Butler. What happens is that movement got kidnapped after the war by the professional middle class in the form of a Hugh Springer and others who started coming into it. The two most important people of it for Adams in the '40s are not going to be middle-class; these were Frank Walcott and Mencea E. Cox.

These two—Walcott and Cox—are going to be [Adams'] two most authentic links to the working class. Until Cox got betrayed in a way; because, when Adams left for the Federal Government Cox was under the impression that he was to succeed Adams. He was told that by Adams.

[Cox] was supposed to be the best at that time. He thought that he was going to be called by the Governor to be Chief Minister and he heard by the radio the Governor announcing the Minister who was Dr. Cummins. When Adams brought his recommendation to the cabinet [Some of his cabinet are said] to have declared that in no circumstances would they serve under a taxi-driver, which Cox was.

Grantley was faced with the decision: would he be fair to Cox and break up the party or hold the party together and be unjust to Cox? What he did was, he thought that the party came before Cox.

MG: So you are saying Slime was that kind of a body.

GL: Slime was that kind of leader. Forms of betrayal imposed upon you, sometimes as the only way of coming to compromises.

MG: Slime is a difficult man to analyse. One, he is around but not present. Then, why don't the people confront him? For example, when the investors come to claim the land, to put out the villagers, Mr. Foster, the shoemaker and the people confront these investors but there is no evidence that they confront Slime.

GL: That is because of the great investment of trust in him. Even though they are for the moment victimized, they would think that down the road he had something else in mind.

Slime is not Adams, but there is a moment in Barbados, not then but later, where no crowd would have confronted Adams on any given thing, even if you could make it as clear as day that it was against them. I don't think there has ever been, including [Errol] Barrow, a Barbadian leader who was held in such total and absolute reverence as Adams was by that generation of poor people, and also whatever few middle class people, because the middle class saw him as their voice talking to the white world. They weren't going to do it for themselves. So all the lawyers and the doctors and upper level schoolteachers (and they wouldn't have been that many), they saw Adams as the man, but it was also the man on the wharf, every section of colour. I remember an old woman telling me there was no way would she vote against Adam.

Long after Adams was dead, there are people who don't

vote for the Barbados Labour Party as such, they would be voting for Adams. And the old woman's explanation was, he took us out of the gutter. There is a big thing in Barbados about Errol Barrow; that is different. There are about two generations who Barrow made it possible to get to the kind of school they went to and to get to university. They are professional now and all that they attribute to Barrow.

It has to do with the expansion of the educational plant and the facilitating of the access to tertiary education. The BLP gets no credit for that whatever they might have thought of doing. That is a Barrow legacy, not even a Democratic Labour Party legacy. But in Adams' time they were not thinking about the tertiary schooling. The secondary school was the tertiary level. But right through the region that was going to happen.

In Jamaica you would have Norman Manley playing a similar role. He was never identified with the working class. He was a genuine patriarch. The labour movement was [Alexander] Bustamante's thing and Manley created a niche there. But between them both they never grew up away from being empire men. Manley was a great patriarch and intellectual. "Busta" was down to the ground. They stayed very much within the [system].

As for the betrayal then, betrayal is sometimes a hard

word. Some people who write on me use it. But I'll tell you, don't do it too often. A lot of people don't realize that the leadership at a certain time which was radicalized by the movement from down below decided at a certain point that they could not move with that movement. They would have to find a way of stopping it or give it new direction.

So in 1953 these are the same people who acted. We were confronted with a very remarkable situation. Politically the most advanced Caribbean territory in 1953 was Guyana. The movement, the People's Progressive Party, was the most politically advanced. Williams hadn't come on the scene yet. That was the combination of Jagan and Burnham; they had this idea about self government.

What was not known for a long time but is known now but few people raise it [is something else about those events]. There was a remarkable collection of men: [including] Eusi Quyana, and they were one step away from independence. The next thing we knew was that the Guyanese constitution was suspended and the ministers dismissed and detained.

Even among West Indians in England there was a virtual outrage everywhere about the suspension of the Guyanese constitution. A free fair election and you dismiss ministers and jail them? All this was not on the part of the British alone. The British on their own wouldn't. But by 1953 this was the height of the cold war. The Americans were not going to tolerate what they saw as a Marxist government going into independence, for they were now responsible for the Caribbean.

The Colonial Office very reluctantly gets involved in what was not their style- to go and suspend constitutions. They therefore consulted two of the major Caribbean leaders for their advice. They knew what they had to do but they needed to speak to [these Caribbean leaders] before they did it. The two they consulted were Norman Manley and Grantley Adams who gave their approval to the suspension of the Guyanese constitution.

MG: This is beginning to sound like Grenada.

GL: This is kept very quiet. In a way, the most advanced political consciousness suffered a regional betrayal. It would happen again, involving Barbados again in 1983 when it was Tom Adams and Eugenia Charles of Dominica in the case of Grenada. So [there is that] theme of betrayal in terms of a leadership that had decided that it wasn't going with the movement.

George Lamming

with Barbadian calypsonian Anthony 'Mighty Gabby' Carter

(photo by Marcille Haynes)

Works Consulted

Allsopp, Richard. *Dictionary of Caribbean English Usage*. New York: Oxford University Press, 1996.

Ashcroft, Bill; Gareth Griffiths; and Helen Tiffin, eds. *The Post-colonial Studies Reader*. London: Routledge, 1995.

Bakhtin, M. M. *The Dialogic Imagination: Four Essays*. Trans. Emerson and M. Holquist. Ed. M. Holquist. Austin Texas: University of Texas Press, 1981.

______. *Rabelais and His World*. Trans. H. Iswolsky. Bloomington, Ind.: Indiana University Press, 1984.

Ball, John Clement. *Satire and the Postcolonial Novel: V. S. Naipaul, Chinua Achebe, Salman Rushdi*. New York: Routlege, 2003.

Barnes, Natasha. "Dancehall Lyricism." *Music, Writing and Cultural Unity in the Caribbean*. Ed. Timothy Reiss. Trenton, N. J.: Africa World Press, 2005. 287-305.

Barriteau, Eudine, ed. *Confronting Power, Theorizing Gender: Interdisciplinary Perspectives in the Caribbean*. Kingston, Jamaica: University of the West Indies Press, 2003.

Barthes, Roland. *Mythologies*. New York: Noonday Press, 1972.

Barton, G. T. *The Prehistory of Barbados*. Bridgetown, Barbados: The Advocate Co., 1953.

Baugh, Eddie. "Belittling the great Tradition, in Good Humour."

The Comic Vision in West Indian Literature. Proc. of the Ninth Conference on West Indian Literature. Ed. Roydon Salick. Port of Spain, Trinidad: n.p., [1993?]. 1-9.

Beckles, Hilary M. and Brian Stoddart, eds. *Liberation Cricket: West Indies Cricket Culture.* Manchester: Manchester University Press, 1995.

Belle, George. "The Struggle for Political Democracy: The 1937 Riots." 150th Anniversary of Emancipation Lecture Series III. National Cultural Foundation. Queen's Park, Bridgetown, Barbados. 17 March 1987.

Belsey, Catherine and Jane Moore, eds. *The Feminist Reader: Essays in Gender and the Politics of Literary Criticism.* London: Macmillan Press, 1989.

Benitez-Rojo, Antonio. "The Repeating Island." *New England Review and Bread Loaf Quarterly* 7.4 (1985): 430-452.

Best, Curwen. *Barbadian Popular Music And The Politics of Caribbean Culture.* New York: AC Inc., 1995.

______. *Roots to Popular Culture: Barbadian Aesthetics: Kamau brathwaite to Hardcore Styles.* London: Macmillan Education, 2001.

______. "Popular/Folk/Creative Arts and the Nation." *The Empowering Impulse: The Nationalist Tradition of Barbados.* Ed. Glenford D. Howe and Don D. Marshall. Barbados: Canoe Press, 2001. 232-255.

Bhabha, Homi K. "Signs Taken For Wonders." *The Postcolonial Studies Reader.* Ed. Bill Ashcroft, Gareth Griffiths, and Helen Tiffin. London: Routledge, 1995. 29-35.

______. *The Location of Culture.* London: Routledge, 1994.

Binford, Leigh. "Revolution: The Central American War Photography of Susan Meiselas and Adam Kufeld." *EIAL Journal Cultura Visual en America*. 9.1 (1998). Estudios Interdisciplinarios de Latina America y El Caribe. 2007. 17 Sept. 2007 http://www.tau.ac.il/eial/Ix_1/binford.html.

Boland, John. *Language and the Quest for Political and Social Identity in the African novel*. Accra, Ghana: Woeli Publishing Services, 1996.

Brathwaite, Edward Kamau. *Rights of Passage*. London: Oxford University Press, 1967.

______. *The Development of Creole Society in Jamaica 1770-1820*. Oxford: Clarendon Press, 1971.

______. New Writing Savacou 1971.

______. *The Arrivants: A New World Trilogy. Rights of Passage, Islands, Masks*. Oxford: Oxford University Press, 1973.

______. *Contradictory Omens: Cultural Diversity and Integration in the Caribbean*. Kingston, Jamaica: Savacou Publications, 1974.

______. *Bajan Culture Report and Plan*. Bridgetown, Barbados: UNESCO, 1979.

______. *History of the Voice*. London: New Beacon Books, 1984.

______. "E.K. Brathwaite." *Three Caribbean Poets On Their Work*. Ed. Victor Chang. Kingston, Jamaica: Institute of Caribbean Studies, U.W.I., 1993.

______. "Jazz and the West Indian Novel." Kamau Bathwaite. *Roots*. USA: Ann Arbor Paperback University of Michigan Press, 1993.

Brathwaite, E. L. "The New West Indian Novelists." *BIM* 32 (1961): 271-280.

Breiner, Lawrence. "How to Behave on Paper: The Savacou Debate." *JWIL* 6.1 (1993): 1-10.

Brewster, Vic. *My Life My Work: Interview with George Lamming*. Spotlight. Caribbean Broadcasting Corporation, Barbados. 9 Nov.

1982.

Brodber, Erna. *Jane and Louisa Will Soon Come Home*. London: New Beacon Books, 1980.

______. *Myal*. London: New Beacon Books, 1988.

Brown, Karen McCarthy. *Mama Lola A Vodun Priest in Brooklyn*. Berkley: University of California Press, 1991.

Brown, Stewart, Mervyn Morris and Gordon Rohlehr, eds. *VOICEPRINT: An Anthology of Oral and Related Poetry From the Caribbean*. Essex: Longman, 1989.

Brown, Stewart. *The Pressures of The Text; Orality and the Telling of Tales*. Birmingham: University of Birmingham, 1995.

Browne, David V.C. "The 1937 Disturbances and Barbadian Nationalism." *The Empowering impulse: The Nationalist Tradition of Barbados*. Ed. Glenford D. Howe and Don D. Marshall. Bridgetown, Barbados: Canoe Press, 2001. 149-164.

Burrowes, Marcia. "The Cloaking of a Heritage: The Barbados Landship." *Contesting Freedom: Control and Resistance in the Post-Emancipation Caribbean*. Ed. Gad Heuman and David V. Trotman. Oxford: Macmillan Caribbean, 2005. 215-234.

Burton, Richard E. *Afro-Creole: Power, Opposition, and Play in the Caribbean*. Ithaca, N.Y.: Cornell University Press, 1997.

Carby, Hazel. *Reconstructing Womanhood: The Emergence of the Afro-American Woman Novelist*. New York: Oxford University Press, 1987.

Castle, Terry. *Masquerade and Civilisation: The Carnivalesque in Eighteenth Century English Culture and Fiction*. California: Standford University Press, 1986.

Chamberlain, Mary. "George Lamming." *West Indian Intellectuals in Britain*. Ed. Bill Schwartz. Manchester: Manchester University Press, 2003. 175-195.

Christian, Barbara. *Black Feminist Criticism: Perspectives on Black Women Writing*. New York: Pergamon Press, 1985.

Cixous, Helen. "The Laugh of the Medusa." *The New French Feminisms: An Anthology*. Ed. Elaine Marks and Isabella de Courtivron. New York: Schocken Books, 1981. 245-264.

Cooper, Carolyn. *Noises In the Blood: Orality, Gender and the Vulgar Body of Jamaican Popular Culture*. Durham,N.C.: Duke University Press, 1985.

______. "Afro-Jamaican Folk Elements in Brodber's *Jane and Louisa Will Soon Come Home*." *Out of the Kumbla: Caribbean Women and Literature*. Ed. Carole Boyce Davies and Elaine Savoury Fido. Trenton, New Jersey: Africa World Press, 1990.

______. "'Lyrical Gun': Metaphor and Role Play in Jamaican Dancehall Culture." *Massachusetts Review*. 35.3-4 (1994): 429-447.

______. "'More Fire': Chanting Down Babylon From Bob Marley to Capelton." *Music, Writing and Cultural Unity in the Caribbean*. Ed. Tim Reiss. Trenton, N. J.: Africa World Press, 2005. 215-236.

Cordle, Edward. "Lizzie Drops Across a Letter in Joes's Possession and is Enraged with Jealousy." *Overheard: A Series of Poems*. Bridgetown, Barbados: C.F. Cole, 1903

Dash, Michael. "In Search of the Lost Body: Redefining the Subject in Caribbean Literature." *Kunappi* 11.1 (1989): 17-26.

Dawes, Kwame. *Towards a New Reggae Aesthetic in Caribbean Writing*. Leeds: Peepal Tree, 1999.

DeBeauvoir, Simone. *The Second Sex*. New York: Alfred Knopf, 1953.

Deitz, Mary. "Introduction: Debating Simone de Beauvoir." *Signs Journal of Women in Culture and Society*. 18.1 (1992): 74-88.

Douglass, Frederick. *Narrative of the Life of Frederick Douglass, an American Slave*. Ed. Huston Baker. 1845. New York: Penguin Books, 1982.

Downes, Aviston. "Sailing from colonial into national waters: A History of the Barbados Landship." *Journal of the Barbados Museum and Historical Society*. XLVI (2000): 93-122.

______. "Searching for Admiral Moses Wood: Oral Tradition and the History of the Landship." *Journal of the Barbados Museum and Historical Society*. XLVIII (2002): 64-78.

Duchrow, Ulrich. *Europe In the World System 1492-1992: Is Justice Possible?* Geneva: World Council of Churches Publications, 1992.

Ellmann, Mary. *Thinking About Women*. New York: Harcourt Brace & World, 1968.

Fannon, Frantz. *The Wretched of the Earth*. London: Penguin Books, 1967.

Farrell, Winston. "Tribute." *Tribute*. Bridgetown, Barbados: n.p., 1996.

Fenigsen, Janina. " 'A Broke-up Mirror': Representing Bajan in Print." *Cultural Anthropology*. 14.1 (1999): 61-87.

Fiske, John. *Understanding Popular Culture*. 1989. London: Routledge, 1991.

Forde, Addinton G. *De Motar-Pestle: A Collection of Barbadian Proverbs*. Bridgetown, Barbados: The National Cultural Foundation of Barbados, 1987.

Francis, Wigmoore. "Nineteenth-and Early-Twentieth Century Perspectives on Women in the Discourses of Radical Black Caribbean Men." *Small Axe* 13 (2003): 116-139.

Freedman, Barbara. *Staging the Gaze: Postmodernism, Psychoanalysis, and Shakespearean Comedy*. Ithaca: Cornell University Press, 1991.

Gates, Henry Louis. *The Signifying Monkey*. Oxford: Oxford University Press, 1988.

Gilbert, Sandra and Susan Gubar. *The Madwoman in the Attic: The Woman Writer and the 19th Century Literary Imagination*. New

Haven: Yale University Press, 1979.

Gill, Margaret D. "A Room of Our Own: Identity and a Post-colonial Feminist Aesthetic in Selected Works by Paule Marshall." MA thesis U. of the West Indies, 1995.

______. "Feminist Discourse and Two Texts by George Lamming." *Confronting Power, Theorizing Gender: Interdisciplinary Perspectives in the Caribbean*. Ed. Eudine Barriteau. Kingston, Jamaica: University of the West Indies Press, 2003.

______. *Alternative Songs From the Kingdom of the Lilies*. Ms. U.W.I. Lib. Bridgetown, Barbados.

______. "Calypso Aesthetic in George Lamming's *In the Castle of My Skin*." *Music, Writing and Cultural Unity in the Caribbean*. Ed. Tim Reiss. Trenton, N. J.: African World Press, 2005. 181-200.

Gilroy, Paul. *The Black Atlantic*. Cambridge: Cambridge University Press, 1993.

Gmelch, George. *Double Passage: The Lives of Caribbean Migrants Abroad and Back home*. Ann Arbor: University of Michigan Press, 1992.

Green, Hazene. "New Voices: The Function of the Imaginative Writer in Society Based on the Work of Four 'Young' Poets in a 'Young' Nation." Caribbean Studies paper U. of the West Indies, 1997.

Greer, Germaine. *The Female Eunuch*. London: Macgibbon, 1970.

Griffith, Glyne. *Deconstruction, Imperialism and the West Indian Novel*. Kingston, Jamaica: The Press University of the West Indies, 1996.

Grimshaw, Anna, ed. *The C. L. R. James Reader*. Oxford: Blackwell Publishers, 1992.

Guy-Sheftall, Beverley, ed. *Words of Fire: An Anthology of African-American Feminist Thought*. New York: The New Press, 1995.

Hall, Douglas. *In Miserable Slavery: Thomas Thistlewood in Jamaica 1750-86*. London: Macmillan Publishers,1989.

Haniff, Yussuff, ed. *Speeches by Errol Barrow*. London: Hansib Publishing Ltd., 1987.

Haynes, Lionel. Personal interview. 16 Jan. 2005.

Hill, Errol. *The Trinidad Carnival*. London: New Beacon Books, 1997.

Hill-Collins, Patricia. *Black Feminist Thought: Knowledge, Consciousness and the Politics of Empowerment*. Perspectives on Gender. 2 Vols. Boston: Hyman, 1990.

Holford, Betty. "Women and Politics." *Advocate Newspaper* [Bridgetown] 7 Oct. 1998: 10.

Holquist, Michael, ed. *The Dialogic Immagination: Four Essays By M.M Bakhtin*. Austin: University of Texas Press, 1981.

Hull, Gloria T. ["Critical Comments"]. Back Cover. Myal. By Erna Brodber. London: New Beacon Books, 1988.

Imoja, Nailah and Jerolynn Thomas. Voices 1. Bridgetown, Barbados: National Cultural Foundation, 1997.

Jacobus, Mary, ed. *Women Writing and Writing about Women*. London: Croom, 1979.

James, C. L. R. *Minty Alley*. London: Secker, 1936.

______. *Mariners, Renegades and Castaways: The Story of Herman Melville and the World We Live In*. New York: n.p., 1953.

______. *Beyond a Boundary*. London: Hutchinson, 1963.

______. "Whitman and Melville." *The C.L.R. James Reader*. Ed. Anna Grimshaw. Oxford: Blackwell, 1992._

Junega, Renu. *Caribbean Transactions*. London: Macmillan Caribbean, 1996.

Jung, Carl. *Memories, Dreams, Reflections: By C.G. Jung*. Ed. Aniela

Jaffe. Trans. Richard Winston and Clara Winston. 1961. New York: Vintage Books, 1965.

Kincaid, Jamaica. *Annie John*. New York: Farrar, 1985.

Knowles, Ronald. *Shakespeare and Carnival: After Bakhtin*. Houndmills: Macmillan, 1998.

Kristeva, Julia. "Word, Dialogue and the Novel." *The Kristeva Reader*. Ed. Toril Moi. Oxford: Basil Blackwell, 1986. 34-61.

Kruks, Sonia. "Gender and Subjectivity: Simone de Beauvoir and Contemporary Feminism." *Signs Journal of Women in Culture and Society*. 18.1 (1992): 89-110.

Lamming, George. *In the Castle of My Skin*. 1953. Essex: Longman, 1979.

______. "Caribbean Literature: The Black Rock of Africa." *Africa Forum*. 1.4 (1966): 32-52.

______. *The Emigrants*. London: Michael Joseph, 1953.

______. *Of Age and Innocence*. London: Michael Joseph, 1958.

______. *Season of Adventure*. London: Michael Joseph, 1960.

______. *The Pleasures of Exile*. London: Michael Joseph, 1960.

______. *Water With Berries*. N.Y.: Longman, 1971.

______. *Natives Of My Person*. N.Y.: Longman, 1972.

______. "Western Education and the Caribbean Intellectual." *Coming Coming Home: Conversations II*. Philipsberg, St Martin: Nehesi, 1995.

______. Personal interview. 02 Aug. 2005.

______. Personal interview. 10 Aug. 2005.

Layne-Clarke, Jeanette. *Bajan Badinage*. Bridgetown, Barbados: Impact Productions, 1993.

______. *Pampalam In De Place: A souvenir Publication Commemorating* the 25*th* *Anniversary of Barbados' Most Popular Comedy Revue.* Bridgetown, Barbados: Impact Productions Limited, 2002.

______. *More Bajan Badinage: An Engaging collection of Dialect Poems.* Bridgetown, Barbados: Impact Productions, 2003.

LiPuma, Edward. "History, Identity and Encompassment: Nation-making in the Solomon Islands." *Identities-Newark.* 4.2 (1997): 213-244.

Liverpool, Hollis. *Rituals of Power and Rebellion: The Carnival Tradition in Trinidad and Tobago.* Chicago: Research Associates School Times, 2001.

Lovelace, Earl. *The Dragon Can't Dance.* Essex: Longman, 1979.

Maginnis, Tara. "Dress in the First and Second Bustle Periods." *The History of Fashion and Dress. Theatre 335 Online Version. The Costumer's Manifesto.* Fairbanks: University of Alaska Fairbanks P, 2007. U of Alaska Fairbanks Press. 17 Sept 2007. http://www.costumes.org/classes/fashiondress/Bus-tleperiods.html.

Marshall, Paule. *Brown Girl, Brownstones.* New York: The feminist Press, 1959.

______. "Language is the only Homeland: Bajan Poets Abroad." Sir Winston Scott Memorial Lecture 19. Frank Collymore Hall, Central Bank of Barbados. Bridgetown, Barbados. 28 Nov. 199.4

______. *The Chosen Place the Timeless People.* USA: Harcourt Brace, 1969.

Marshall, Trevor, Peggy McGeary and Grace Thompson. *Folk Songs of Barbados.* Kingston, Jamaica: Ian Randall, 1996.

Marshall, Trevor. "Notes on the History and Evolution of Calypso in Barbados." Seminar on the Calypso. ISER/UWI Calypso Research Project. U.W.I., Port of Spain, Trinidad. 10-17 Jan. 1986.

McDougall, Russell. "The Body as Cultural Signifier." *The Postcolonial*

Studies Reader. Ed. Bill Ashcroft, Gareth Griffiths and Helen Tiffin. London: Routledge, 1995. 336-340.

McWatt, Mark. "Inventing Ancestors: Strategies for Identity and Belonging in Selected Guyanese Writing." 15th Annual Conference on West Indian Literature. St Augustine Campus, UWI.,1996.

Melville, Preston. Personal interview. 2 July 2005.

Millett, Kate. *Sexual Politics*. London: Virago, 1977.

Moi, Toril. *Sexual/Textual Politics: Feminist Literary Theory*. London: Mathuen, 1985.

______, ed. *The Kristeva Reader*. Oxford: Basil Blackwell, 1986.

Morris, Pam, ed. *The Bakhtin Reader: Selected Writings of Bakhtin, Medvedev, Voloshinov*. London: Edward Arnold, 1994.

Morrison, Toni. *Beloved*. London: Pan Books, 1988.

Nye, Andrea. *Feminist Theory and the Philosophies of Man*. New York: Routledge, 1989.

Ocallaghan, Evelyn. *Woman Version: Theoretical Approaches to West Indian Fiction by Women*. London: Macmillan Caribbean, 1993.

Paquet, Sandra Pouchet. *The Novels of George Lamming*. London: Heinemann, 1982.

______. "The Fifties." *West Indian Literature*. Ed. Bruce King. 2nd ed. London: Macmillan Education, 1995. 51-62.

Ramchand, Kenneth. *An Introduction to the Study of West Indian Literature*. Middlesex: Nelson Caribbean, 1976.

______. *The West Indian Novel and its Background*. London: Faber, 1970.

Reiss, Timothy, ed. *Geography of A Soul: Emerging Perspectives on Kamau Brathwaite*. New Jersey: Africa World Press, 2001.

______, ed. *Music, Writing and Cultural Unity in the Caribbean*.

Trenton, N. J.: Africa World Press, 2005.

Rhys, Jean. *Wide Sargasso Sea*. London: Hodder, 1989.

Rohlehr, Gordon. Introduction. "The Shape of that Hurt." *Voiceprint*. Ed. Stewart Brown, Mervyn Morris and Gordon Rohlehr. Kingston, Jamaica: Longman, 1989. 1-23.

______. *Calypso and Society in Pre-Independence Trinidad*. Port of Spain, Trinidad: n.p., 1990.

______. *My Strangled City and Other Essays*. Port of Spain, Trinidad: Longman, 1992.

______. "Drum and Minuet: Music, Masquerade, and the Mulatto of Style." *Music, Writing and Cultural Unity in the Caribbean*. Ed. Tim Reiss. Trenton, N.J.: Africa World Press, 2005. 149-179.

Russo, Mary. *The Female Grotesque: Risk, Excess and Modernity*. New York: Routledge, 1995.

St, John, Bruce. Introduction to Bruce St. John's first public reading of Pains held at the Common Room of the Centre for Multiracial Studies, June 21, 1971.

Savory, Elaine. "Returning to Sycorax/Prospero's Response: Kamau Brathwaite's Word Journey." *The Art of Kamau Brathwaite*. Ed. Stewart Brown. Wales: Seren, 1995. 211-230.

Scott, David. "The Sovereignty of the Imagination: An Interview with George Lamming." *Small Axe*. 12 (2002): 72-200.

Searle, Chris. "Race before Cricket: Cricket, Empire, and the White Rose." *Race and Class*. 31.3 (1990): 343-345.

Showalter, Elaine. *A Literature of Their Own: British Women Novelists from Bronte to Leesing*. Princeton: Princeton University Press, 1977.

Smith, Paul. *Discerning the Subject*. Minneapolis: University of

Minnesota Press, 1988.

Spivak, Gayatri. "Three Women's Texts and a Critique of Imperialism." *The Post-colonial Studies Reader.* Ed. Bill Ashcroft, Gareth Griffiths, Helen Tiffin. London: Routledge, 1985. 36-44.

Thomas, Dylan. *Collected Poems: 1934-1952.* London:Everyman's Library, 1952.

Thomas, J. J. *The Theory and Practice of Creole Grammar.* London: New Beacon,

Thompson, Tony. Personal interview. 27 Oct. 2005.

Thorpe, Marjorie. Introduction. *The Wine of Astonishment.* By Earl Lovelace. 1982. London: Heinemann, 1986.

Walcott, Derek. "The Light of the World." *The Arkansas Testament.* New York: Farrar, 1987. 48-51.

Warner, K. Q. *Trinidad Calypso: A Study of the Calypso as Oral Literature.* Washington: Three continents Press, 1982.

Wiles, David. "The Carnivalesque in *A Midsummer Night's Dream.*" *Shakespeare and Carnival.* Ed. Ronald Knowles. Houndmills: Macmillan, 1998. 61-82.

Williams, David. "Rereading Our Classics: *In the Castle of My Skin* and *Lonely Londoners.*" *Gendered Realities: Essays in Caribbean Thought.* Ed. Patricia Mohammed. Kingston, Jamaica: University of the West Indies Press, 2002. 291-296.

Woolf, Virginia. *A Room of One's Own.* Florida: HBJ, 1989.